T0128428

HOMESPUN PRAYERS

Conversations with God

LINDA SMOCK

WESTBOW
PRESS®
A DIVISION OF THOMAS NELSON
& ZONDERVAN

WestBow Press books may be ordered through booksellers or by contacting:

WestBow Press
A Division of Thomas Nelson & Zondervan
1663 Liberty Drive
Bloomington, IN 47403
www.westbowpress.com
844-714-3454

ISBN: 978-1-6642-8270-4 (sc)
ISBN: 978-1-6642-8268-1 (hc)
ISBN: 978-1-6642-8269-8 (e)

Library of Congress Control Number: 2022920348

Print information available on the last page.

WestBow Press rev. date: 11/23/2022

Dedicatory Prayer

Lord God, since this is a book of prayers, please use it as my offer of a living sacrifice to You. Please use Your Holy Spirit to bless the readers as they participate in a few of the conversations You and I have had over the last year.

Acknowledgements

Where do I start with appreciation? There are so many people to whom I need to say a huge "Thank you" but I think the greatest appreciation and thanks goes to our Lord and Savior Jesus Christ, who is the source of our grace and who opened up the throne room of heaven in a way that allows each of us to go before the Father with our most private thoughts and feelings, our requests, and our questions. God knows what we are thinking so why not state it? It helps us when we do. I thank Jesus and I thank God for that open throne room and their listening ears and hearts full of love for us. What's more – they hung the moon, giving us idiom to use as we talk!

Thanks also to four ladies who have graciously given of their time to not only the content of this book, but three previous books. Each one reviews a portion of my writings with each piece reviewed by at least two of them. These sisters-in-Christ are Barb Admire, Dolores Hayman, Sandy Peeples, and Kym Samek. They are faithful friends through thick and thin.

Teachers and ministers have played a big role in teaching me to think, study, and pray about the meaning of scriptures. These include but are not limited to Gayle Crowe, Joel Harper, Jim Shannon, Joe Stephens, and George Welty. Although I've never met them, people like Tony Evans, Kyle Idleman, Max Lucado, Beth Moore, Andy Stanley, Charles Stanley, Chuck Swindoll, and Sarah Young have taught me much through their books, videos, radio and podcast lessons. There are many more I could list, but those are the ones I've listened to the most and read many of their books and resources. They've taught me to get my rear in gear and to transfer the knowledge I've gained from my head to my heart and actions.

Whether you start this book with your cup half empty or half full, may you fill your cup to overflowing as you pray these prayers with me.

Introduction

I've read that in Paul's letters to the churches, sixty-eight of the verses are prayers. I wonder how much of his day was spent in prayer? I don't know, but I do know that most of those sixty-eight verses focus on praying for others and not for himself, although he does ask the readers to pray for him.

I wish I were half as good at praying as people think I am. One thing I've come to realize is that the prayers I write are much more from my heart than routine prayers that I say at mealtime, when I get up, or when I prepare to sleep. I also find that "arrow" prayers are common – brief sentences or even just the words, "Help, Lord" - shot up to God are effective and help in that quest to "pray continually" as Paul admonishes us to do (I Thessalonians 5:16-18).

So why have I written these one hundred prayers? First, for me. My prayer life is more effective when I write my prayers. Second, for God who should have been first, but if I'm honest, He's not always. Third, for you, the reader. I hope they will help you (and me) to develop better prayer habits, to use time with God for conversations, just as we do in any healthy relationship that we have, including family, fellow Christians, neighbors, co-workers, and best friends. In our relationships with these people, our conversations vary. They may be brief chats, long and deep questioning, heated discussions, casual observations, or many other forms. Can conversing with God be the same? I think so, and I hope these chats, questions, discussions, and observations will help all of us develop intimacy with our Lord and Savior.

Idioms and colloquial sayings are quite common in our society and God has given me one for each of these prayers. Often they just come to mind, but sometimes I research in an effort to find the right one. I keep a list of them and occasionally use the same ones I've used in previous books. It's fun to research their background and origin as I prepare to use them.

Most of my prayers are private, never shared with anyone except God. In fact, that's true of most folks – their thoughts and prayers are private. This book is a glimpse into the private conversations I have had with God, usually about a scripture He's provided us, but sometimes over an issue in the news, or some interest of mine that is peaked by something that has occurred such as a chat with a friend.

One of the great things about having conversations with God is that He is a good listener. I suspect He would like me to also be a good listener. In some of these prayers, I include what I think God is saying to me while in others, I'm left hanging without a clear answer, and want to tell God His answers are about as clear as mud. I would prefer that God had given me an answer that I could grasp, but His timing is better than mine, and so I await the answer He will provide in His perfect timing.

It is my hope and prayer that God will use these conversations to help both you and me to grow in our relationship with Him, and to come to know Him, to believe Him, not just believe in Him. If we are not already in love with Him, may we fall head over heels in love with Him.

Ain't Over till the
Fat Lady Sings

Zacharias and Elizabeth were godly folk, careful
to obey all of God's laws in spirit as well as in
letter. But they had no children, for Elizabeth was
barren; and now they were both very old.

—Luke 1:6–7 (TLB)

Lord, this phrase about opera has been used since 1978, but
it could have been used back when Zacharias and Elizabeth
were waiting for a baby. I don't know how old they were, but
possibly over fifty, even in their seventies, but who knows? Doesn't
matter, does it, Lord? The opera was not over; the fat lady had
not sung; You still had plans. And You timed it well, even though
back when they were young, they were probably upset that they
didn't have a child, possibly even wanted a big bunch of children
like their friends and neighbors had. They waited and waited,
waited and waited, and may have given up hope.

Suddenly, You show up—and so does a baby. A little boy,
and You promise that the little boy will be something special,
and You filled him with the Holy Spirit when he was born (Luke

1

1:15). The waiting was worth it. In their old age, they watched a little boy develop into a young man. Did they live long enough to see what he did for Your kingdom? I don't know, but I hope they didn't live long enough to see what King Herod did to him later during the ministry of Jesus.

Waiting. I don't like it when it is something I really want. I can imagine how long that wait must have felt to Zacharias and Elizabeth. Help me to have faith and hang on with both hands as I wait for You to answer prayers and help me have faith that Your timing is perfect. The fat lady will sing at Your perfect timing. Through my Savior Jesus, who waited thirty years to start His ministry, I ask this.

All Over but the Shouting

Now thanks be to God for His Gift, [precious] beyond telling [His indescribable, inexpressible, free Gift].

—2 Corinthians 9:15 (AMPC)

About the ninth hour Jesus cried out with a loud [agonized] voice, "Eli, Eli, lama sabachthani?" that is, "My God, My God, why have You forsaken Me?"

—Matthew 27:46 (AMP)

You gave Your life, Jesus. You died. Did You shout "Hallelujah" when You were back in heaven? Were You thrilled to be back in Your own home, finished with Your time on earth and those three days in the grave? Was it all over but the shouting?

I cannot imagine what it must have been like to leave heaven, come to earth, spend thirty-three years among people who were disrespectful, lacking faith and trust, confused, and cruel to You. Thankfully, there were some who treated You well most of the

3

time. But in the scheme of things, it was just a few, and they had their doubts.

There were the twelve whom You called to be Your apostles. You taught them, trusted them with healing people, and asked them to pray for You. Most of the time, they did well with what You asked them to do. Before Your death, however, they had their doubts and faltered in their faith. Peter denied You three times, some avoided the sight of the cross so they would not see You suffer or be likely to go up on a cross themselves, and we all know that Judas betrayed You.

Your love for them and for all of us became evident as You allowed those Roman soldiers to lead You to the cross of crucifixion, allowed Satan to appear to win, and allowed the apostles to walk away each in their own way. Lord, it was not evident to them at that time, but in hindsight, they saw it perfectly. They were not shouting, "Hallelujah" as You hung on that cross, but they were when You appeared in that room without coming through a door or window.

And there were the masses of people. One day they lined the streets with palm branches, proclaiming You as King. Some of them were fickle and were in the crowd that shouted, "Crucify Him" a few days later. How many of them were in the thousands who were baptized as recorded in the book of Acts? Did they shout "Hallelujah" when they realized You were resurrected, just as You had said You would be?

I have so many questions, Lord, but I suspect when I get to heaven, I won't care. I'll be thrilled to be with You, and I'll be shouting, "Hallelujah" to Jesus my Savior and Lord. What a savior You are, giving me something for which to shout "Hallelujah" every day of my life—salvation.

As Paul said, "Thanks be to God." Amen.

An Ace up Your Sleeve

> Let me show you what the man who comes to me, hears what I have to say, and puts it into practice, is really like. He is like a man building a house, who dug down to rock-bottom and laid the foundation of his house upon it. Then when the flood came and floodwater swept down upon that house, it could not shift it because it was properly built. But the man who hears me and does nothing about it is like a man who built his house with its foundation upon the soft earth. When the floodwater swept down upon it, it collapsed and the whole house crashed down in ruins.
>
> —John 6:47–49 (J. B. Phillips New Testament)

I trust the building I live in to stand through storms, dear God. I did not see it under construction, but I know about the codes that had to be met and the inspectors who checked to be sure it was meeting the city's criteria. I don't think about it very often, but now and then, when I hear of a building that came crashing down, I wonder about the last time my building was checked … and then I forget again, trusting that it will stand. I think of those building codes and inspections as an ace up my sleeve, assuring me that all is well.

Life is that way too, Lord. I've got an ace up my sleeve—You. You are my foundation, built on solid rock, not shifting sand. I trust Your way, Your grace, and Your salvation; thus, I don't worry about death. Oh, I've planned for what is to happen here on earth when I transition to heaven, but I don't focus and spend time worrying about where I'll be when my physical body dies … most of the time. But just like with the building I live in, now and then something happens that reminds me I am not worthy. The doubts creep in. Thankfully, You remind me of my solid foundation in You, and I remember to trust You for my transition to heaven, not my own efforts. Your grace is sufficient, and I soon quit worrying about the future, because I've got an ace up my sleeve.

Through my foundation, Jesus (my ace up my sleeve), I thank You.

Ask No Questions

Study to shew thyself approved unto God, a workman that needeth not to be ashamed, rightly dividing the word of truth.

—2 Timothy 2:15 (KJV)

Study: devote time to; give attention to; focus on; acquire knowledge; investigate; analyze; think about.

L ord, many of us memorized this scripture as a child, but have we applied it? Have we questioned what we were taught, or have we just accepted it? Were we told to ask no questions, or did we just assume we should ask no questions and go along with what we were taught? If we questioned, were those questions welcomed, or were we shamed for asking them? Would You ever tell us to ask no questions? I don't think so—You welcomed the questions of Your disciples. You questioned the priests when You were twelve years old. You wanted to understand the scriptures enough to question—and if I'm to be like You, then I also need to ask questions and study.

Lord, forgive us for our failure to study, our reliance upon the study done by others. Help us to devote time to topics we need to know more about. Help us investigate. Help us meditate. Help us focus on Your Word and give attention to Your Holy Spirit. Thank You.

Asleep at the Wheel/Switch

Now the Berean Jews were of more noble character than those in Thessalonica, for they received the message with great eagerness and examined the Scriptures every day to see if what Paul said was true. As a result, many of them believed, as did also a number of prominent Greek women and many Greek men.

—Acts 17:11–12 (NIV)

Lord, I've been asleep at the wheel. I've read this scripture all my life. As a child, I heard it preached and was told I, too, needed to search the scripture. But You know well I never once thought about what scriptures the Bereans were reading. As a child, I pictured them with Bibles open, reading and studying, but alas, the New Testament was not even written, and the Old Testament was rare in homes. Most had to go to the synagogue to see a copy, and many could not read. So how did they study it? I'm glad my friend asked me what they were studying and got me to thinking.

I notice that they first "received the message." I picture Paul in the synagogue telling them about Jesus as the fulfillment of scripture. They listened, captivated, knowing that the scrolls would tell them the clues they needed to determine if Paul was telling the truth. They "received" by listening "with eagerness." They must have been curious, wanting to know more. They discussed and talked among themselves.

Next, they "examined the scriptures every day." That took some commitment, Lord. They had to go to the synagogue every day to have the Old Testament scriptures to read—and wait until someone who could read came. Did some go daily, or did different ones go on various days? Did Paul stay around to read for them? How did they examine? Did they ask the reader to look for certain things? Did they look for the prophesies about the King coming as an infant? Did they study all the prophesies, trying to put two and two together to figure out if what Paul was telling them was true? What questions were they asking? One thing I know: they were not asleep at the wheel. It took focus to "examine" what was written on a scroll.

I also notice that "belief" followed. Paul's teachings didn't go in one ear and out the other. They stuck—not because they were his words but because they examined, studied, and sought for the truth. Two plus two made four. They believed.

Lord, like I said before, I'm guilty. I've been asleep at the wheel. Too often, I've just accepted what I was taught and never really studied to find out if it was true or not. Oh, I may have looked at the scriptures that teachers gave me in isolation, assuming (and having more faith in the teachers than in Your inspired word) that they had done the study and reached the right conclusion. But I didn't try to find the truth for myself. I let the blind lead the blind. I was asleep at the wheel. Forgive me.

Lord, help me to be like the Bereans—committed to examining Your word, not to prove what I've been taught, but to look for You and Your will, Your way, Your love. You are truth. Forgive my failures.

Back on Her Feet

Is anyone among you suffering? He should keep on praying about it. And those who have reason to be thankful should continually be singing praises to the Lord.

Is anyone sick? He should call for the elders of the church and they should pray over him and pour a little oil upon him, calling on the Lord to heal him. And their prayer, if offered in faith, will heal him, for the Lord will make him well; and if his sickness was caused by some sin, the Lord will forgive him.

—James 5:13–15 (Living Bible)

Father God and Great Physician, I have so many friends who are sick, who need and want to get back on their feet. Most seem to either have heart problems or cancer, but there are other problems too. You tell us to pray, and we do. You also say it needs to be in faith. Do we lack faith? Lack faith in You or in our doctors? We know You created the heavens, and You created us. We believe You can heal. We believe You are sovereign and have the ultimate plan in Your hands. How do we find the healthy balance in our faith, enough to trust You to get our friends and loved ones back up on their feet but allowing Your sovereign will to reign supreme?

I don't know, Lord, but I still ask that my friend's infusions this month be easier on her body, that she can have them without side effects or minimal side effects. I ask that they target the cancer cells that need to be destroyed and that they cause them to die and be eliminated from her body. I ask that You help her to have a cheerful outlook about the benefits as she moves forward with these treatments. Use her doctors to do what is best for her body that You may use her in future years to help others love You. Our trust is in You.

For my friend with heart disease, who awaits a heart transplant, what should I ask? To get a heart transplant, someone else must die. Yet we know it happens with accidents, and one of those good healthy hearts could give him several more years of life. He's been a wonderful servant during his time on this earth, and many of us want him to keep living and using his talents. Would you use the upcoming heart transplant to repair his body and give him the health needed to serve You until he becomes an old man? He wants to be back on his feet. Our trust is in You.

There's the baby with the birth defect in her heart too, Lord. I don't understand why these things happen. I want that little heart to be perfect, to be whole, so she can grow up on her feet loving and serving You. Would You just heal her? I want You to snap Your fingers and all be right. I want her mom and dad to never have to worry about what will happen if they can't pay the bills because of the expenses of medical care for her, with multiple surgeries. It doesn't seem like that is what is going to happen. It seems like it is going to take lots of surgeries at a hospital many hours from their home with expenses ongoing. People with good-paying jobs can't afford that. That's why I just want You to snap Your fingers and make it right. If that is not Your will, help us all to accept Your will and Your process of healing, Your use of the medical community, the financial help of their church community and their neighbors. Help us to have good attitudes through whatever process You use because we believe You can use even dreadful things to create good. Our trust is in You.

One more thing, Lord. My friend's teen son says he doesn't want to live. His mom's heart is breaking. Would You please help him feel Your love and Your presence and know that he is loved by his parents, grandparents, and siblings? Give him reason and purpose for living. Our trust is in You.

I could keep going, Lord. I know hundreds of folks sick, emotionally distraught, lonely, fighting the challenges of living on earth. Help us each as You see fit. We want to be up on our feet, putting one foot in front of the other, having strength and courage to face every trial that comes our way. Our trust is in You.

Back to the Wall

> When you harvest the crops of your land, do not gather *the grain* all the way to the edges of your fields or pick up what was overlooked during the *first round of* harvesting. *Likewise* do not strip the vines bare in your vineyard or gather the fallen grapes. Leave the fallen fruit and some grapes on the vine for the poor and strangers *living among you*; for I am the Eternal your God.
>
> —Leviticus 19:9–10 (The Voice)

Lord, I know people whose backs are to the wall. They just don't have enough money to make it to the next paycheck. They work; they try. But ends don't meet. So how do I help them?

You told the Israelites that they were to leave the edges of their fields available for folks with their backs to the wall to gather the grain and to leave fruit available for them to gather. How do we do this in our modern-day society where very few of us are farmers? Most of us don't even have gardens. Guide us to creative ways of helping our fellow man.

Thank You for the people who are being creative in helping others, Lord. Some vegetable stands give their extra vegetables and fruits to churches to create vegetarian meals for those in need. Some grocery stores give their canned foods that are close to the sell-date expiration to food pantries. I know a lady who has a community garden and only grows vegetables for the neighboring community center where people gather for the groceries available at little or no cost to them. The company from which I get my chemo pills has a program available to help the poor get their drugs without copays if they can't afford the copay. I know a man who teaches people to budget and use their available money more wisely, thus using his talent to help others. A friend who is a dentist has taken care of many people with toothaches without charging.

Thank You, Lord, for these people, who are leaving grain at the edges of their fields, leaving fruit on the ground. They are helping those whose backs are against the wall. Show me how You want me to be creative in my provision for those whose backs are against the wall.

Backed into a Corner

My God. Rescue me from my enemies,
    defend me from these mutineers.
Rescue me from their dirty tricks,
    save me from their hit men.
Desperadoes have ganged up on me,
    they're hiding in ambush for me.
I did nothing to deserve this, GOD,
    crossed no one, wronged no one.
All the same, they're after me,
    determined to get me.
Wake up and see for yourself. You're GOD,
GOD-of-Angel-Armies, Israel's God.
Get on the job and take care of these pagans,
    don't be soft on these hard cases.
            —Psalm 59:1–5 (The Message)

Was David a teenager when he wrote this, Lord? Some folks believe he was trying to escape from King Saul who was jealous and angry. I don't think of any teenagers that I know who would talk with You this way. Neither do I know any young adults who would. Come to think of it, I don't know anyone any age who feels comfortable talking this way to You.

He sure makes it sound like he was backed into a corner, fearing for his life, knowing people wanted to kill him. Did King Saul have a bounty out for his head? He lied to his soldiers who were trying to capture and kill David. Were there soldiers who were loyal to King Saul and would do what he said, no matter what? Were they brainwashed? Where was David hiding? There are lots of caves in those mountains around Jerusalem and throughout Israel. Which ones did he use to avoid being slain?

Another question, Lord: How had David developed such strong faith in You? Did his parents train him in that way? Had his Dad Jesse trained him in Your ways, helped him develop a deep relationship with You? Had his unnamed mother been influential in developing that faith? Or maybe his grandparents Boaz and Ruth? Did it come from spending so much time alone with only You and the sheep with whom to talk?

More importantly, Lord, how do I react when I'm backed into a corner? Do I fight? Do I flee? Do I deny and avoid? Do I express the kind of faith that David expressed? What is my relationship with You, and how do I react when I feel cornered? My faith seems like a mustard seed compared to David, no matter what his age. History indicates he was a lot younger than me, an older teenager or young adult. The young folks I know now don't write prayers out very often if ever. Do I need to be training them to do so?

Oh, Lord, I'm full of questions. I thank You that I'm not backed into a corner physically and ask You to guide me to deeper faith so that I can relate to You as David did when I get emotionally backed into a corner. Help my unbelief to grow so that I express faith and trust in You as David did.

And me? I'm singing your prowess,
shouting at dawn your largesse,
For you've been a safe place for me,
a good place to hide.
Strong God, I'm watching you do it,
I can always count on you—
God, my dependable love.
—Psalm 59:16–17 (The Message)

Bad Blood between Them

First of all, I ask that you pray for all people. Ask God to bless them and give them what they need. And give thanks. You should pray for rulers and for all who have authority. Pray for these leaders so that we can live quiet and peaceful lives—lives full of devotion to God and respect for him. This is good and pleases God our Savior.
—1 Timothy 2:1–3 (Easy-to-Read Version)

Lord, there is bad blood between some of our politicians. They appear to hold grudges. Some are not willing to compromise. They insult. They call coworkers ugly names. They don't believe the same things, and they act childishly for the media wanting to get their own way.

Would You bless them with what they need? I don't know what they need specifically, but it seems like a good dose of common sense would help. Perhaps a better attitude about You and a desire to do what is right in Your sight, not trying to please constituents and get reelected? Do they need a willingness to compromise? If they are acting selfishly, help them to become selfless instead. Many of them need You—or at least appear to. Help them find You by whatever means You know will work with each.

You also tell me to give thanks for them. So, thank You. Thank You for their willingness to run for election. That must be incredibly stressful, whether they are at the local, state, or national level. Thank You that they make lots of sacrifices for us—often their time, money, energy, or health. Thank You that they have commitments and opinions that help them in their decisions. Thank You for the training they have had for their various roles, including training in law, in law enforcement, in political science, in medicine, and many other occupations. Thank You for the sacrifices their families make also.

Lord, we pray for all those who have authority. Not all are elected politicians. Some are appointed to their jobs. Some with authority are our supervisors, our bosses. Some are our elders, pastors, ministers. Some are our parents. Some are teachers and principals, school presidents, or other educational roles. The list goes on and on. They need Your help, each in their individual ways. Bless them as You see fit.

We also pray that our leaders, whether elected or appointed, whether we personally know them or not, can live quiet and peaceful lives—lives full of devotion to You and respect for You. Let there be good blood between You and them, and no bad blood between them and others in leadership. Thank You that they care for the people in their authority.

Barking up the Wrong Tree

Be therefore imitators of God, as beloved children. Walk in love, even as Christ also loved us and gave himself up for us, an offering and a sacrifice to God for a sweet-smelling fragrance.
        —Ephesians 5:1–2 (World English Bible)

I'm confused, Lord. Have I been barking up the wrong tree all these years? I've always thought of sacrifices as things I gave up, just as You, Jesus, gave up Your breath of life for me. But now I hear Ann Voskamp describe it as "to come closer." I think what she's saying is that to come close to You, to crawl up into Your lap and hug You, I've got to let go of my baggage and my stuff, got to come with arms outstretched, hands empty, heart surrendered. Anything that I carry creates a barrier between us. I grow close to You by surrendering all to You.

I like control, Lord. I like to feel like my personal life is in my control. I like to think that all that stuff is mine—home, auto, money in the bank, plants on the porch. I like to feel that my health is under my control. But honestly, none of it is under my control. I just try to make it be. Yes, by trying, I'm barking up the wrong tree.

So, how can I change and bark up the right tree? How do I come closer to You? Give up control. Give up pretending. Give up hypocrisy. Lay it all at Your feet and hop up in Your lap for a big bear hug. So far, Lord, that's come in small steps for me. Sometimes I lay something at Your feet and soon find I've picked it back up without even realizing it. But if I am carrying it, my arms are not outstretched, not ready to have You welcome me to Your lap, where Your arms are always ready to embrace me.

Lord, nudge me when You hear me barking up the wrong tree. Give me reminders to surrender all to You, dropping my burdens at Your feet, so that my arms are open, and there are no barriers between You and me. Thank You.

Be There with Bells On

God saved you by his grace when you believed. And you can't take credit for this; it is a gift from God. Salvation is not a reward for the good things we have done, so none of us can boast about it. For we are God's masterpiece. He has created us anew in Christ Jesus, so we can do the good things he planned for us long ago.
—Ephesians 2:8–10 (New Living Translation)

To be considered Your masterpiece Wow! I've got my bells on, Lord, celebrating how great You think I am.

To think that You made each of us, are crafting us into masterpieces—that's amazing. You crafted the Grand Canyon, Niagara Falls, White Sands, the Smoky Mountains ... wonderful landscapes that leave us in awe. Those are worthy of celebrating with our bells on.

But we are also in awe to think that You are crafting us into beautiful and wonderful humans who declare Your glory just as the beauty of nature sings Your praises.

It's easy to look at newborns and think of them being masterpieces. Those little fingers are so perfectly formed, the skin so smooth, and those eyes lock with ours. We marvel. We celebrate those births with bells on. But to think of sinful adults as Your masterpieces is hard, Lord. Yet You say that we are. We are created anew in Jesus when we accept Him as Lord and Savior. We become a newborn all over again.

You also say You've planned good works for those of us who are Your masterpieces. You don't expect us to sit around playing games or watching television all day long. You've got things You want us to do. You don't list them, but I'm thinking about the time You said You wanted us to help our fellow Christians (Galatians 6:8–10), the many times You mentioned helping the poor (such as Proverbs 19:17), and the time You had Paul thank the Philippians for assisting him as a missionary (Philippians 4:15). There's always good work available to do—many volunteer opportunities. What's more, people put their bells on when we volunteer.

Thank You, Master, who creates masterpieces. You've done wonderful things, and You are still doing remarkable things including making us into masterpieces. You are amazing, and we will gladly be there with our bells on to celebrate You. You are worthy.

Beggars Can't Be Choosers

Then, as he was approaching Jericho, it happened that there was a blind man sitting by the roadside, begging. He heard the crowd passing and enquired what it was all about. And they told him, "Jesus the man from Nazareth is going past you." So, he shouted out, "Jesus, Son of David, have pity on me." Those who were in front tried to hush his cries. But that made him call out all the more, "Son of David, have pity on me." So Jesus stood quite still and ordered the man to be brought to him. And when he was quite close, he said to him, "What do you want me to do for you?" "Lord, make me see again," he cried. "You can see again. Your faith has cured you," returned Jesus. And his sight was restored at once, and he followed Jesus, praising God. All the people who saw it thanked God too.

—Luke 18:35–43 (J. B. Phillips
New Testament)

Beggars can be choosers, Lord. You allowed this man to be a chooser, and he started as a beggar. I can just imagine him by the side of the road near Jericho, listening intently to know what was going on around him, when there was a chance to ask for something, talking to other beggars to get the lay of the land, the local news and gossip. I imagine, Lord, that You were one of the few that took the time to talk with him, to give him even the time of day. The people were trying to hush him, to protect You from him, but You took the time to look at him, to understand him as a person, and asked those around him to bring him to You, knowing he could not see to come to You. You were kind, gentle, loving—not like other rabbis that had passed by. You were the man he had heard about, and he wanted Your help.

When You asked him what he wanted, he was quick to answer—he wanted to see. So You cured whatever was wrong with his eyes, and he could see. What did he do then? He followed You. It's possible all his earthly belongings were there by the side of the road, but he didn't go back for them. He didn't run to his family to tell them. He *followed You*. He *praised You*. His gratitude and enthusiasm were so great that those around him thanked God also.

What do You want me to learn from this story, Lord? The first thing that comes to my mind is that I need to also follow You with enthusiasm and gratitude, and I need to praise You. How will those around me react? There's no guarantee that they will thank and praise You, but there is a good chance.

Yes, we are all beggars—begging for Your mercy. As beggars, we have a choice. We can seek You and be rewarded in ways beyond our imagination. Your blessings will flow. I thank You for giving us that choice and for blessing us when we choose to follow You.

Best Things Come in Small Packages

Immediately the boy's father exclaimed, "I do believe; help me overcome my unbelief."
—Mark 9:24 (New International Version)

He replied, "Because you have so little faith. Truly I tell you, if you have faith as small as a mustard seed, you can say to this mountain, 'Move from here to there,' and it will move. Nothing will be impossible for you."
—Matthew 17:20 (New International Version)

I'm often amazed, Lord, by little things. Large packages may hold wonderful things, but often the small packages hold the things of greatest value. But what about small packages of faith and small packages of humility? Are You happy with those or do You want us to have large packages of them?

To me, Lord, that little boy's father had some faith. He asked You to heal his son "if You can." Then he asked for more faith. You obviously were pleased with that faith, no matter what size it was. You healed that little boy. You also tell us that even faith as small as a mustard seed is good. That is small, a little package, which makes You happy. Faith, no matter the size, is pleasing to You. As we express and share it, it grows, and soon that package gets a little bigger.

Humility. Now that's a tough one for us humans, Lord. The father who brought his son who was having convulsions to You must have been humbled by his son's behavior, perhaps embarrassed by it. He was desperate for help, and he sought You out in that crowd. When You questioned him, he humbly asked for more faith. He had been through a lot with his little boy. You don't really mention humility in the story in Mark 9, but it seems to me that humility and faith go hand in hand. Am I right, Lord?

It seems to me, Jesus, that the package size does not matter all that much when it comes to faith and humility. You respond to whatever the size. That's wonderful. Thank You.

Between a Rock
and a Hard Place

> When Jesus finished saying these things, he told
> his disciples, "You know that Passover comes in
> two days. That's when the Son of Man will be
> betrayed and handed over for crucifixion."
> —Matthew 26:2 (The Message)

Sounds like You were between a rock and a hard place, Lord.
You managed it so differently than I would have.

You told Your apostles (at least eleven of the twelve), whom
You had recruited, trained, and was preparing to leave Your
kingdom work to, that You would be dying in two days. They each
reacted in their own way. Judas went off and accepted thirty silver
coins in payment for leading You to the officials who would kill
You. Peter boastfully proclaimed he would never forsake You and
promptly denied he knew You three times. You took Peter, James,
and John farther into Gethsemane to pray for You, and they fell
asleep. Later, the remainder of them slipped away, possibly not
wanting to be seen for fear they too might be on a cross. Well,

not all of them. John seemed to have slipped in and tracked what was going on.

There You were, knowing You were going to die, wanting support and compassion, yet not receiving any from those eleven guys. The rock was on one side, and a hard place was on the other. You were being squeezed. It must have been an awful predicament to be in. You wanted them to live up to Your standard, to what You had taught them, to accept some responsibility and to pray for You in this horrible time. They gave in to their sleepiness and let You down.

How did You react? You didn't get angry, didn't yell at them. Oh, You did express Your disappointment, but then You encouraged them to get up and go with You as Judas approached You to betray You.

Those guys did not live up to Your standard. How do I react when people don't live up to my standard? I think of lots of failures over the years, Lord—failures with my parents and brother, failures with my husband, failures with extended family, failures in my career, failures in my friendships and community. When I've been between the rock and the hard place, I didn't react as graciously as You did. When they didn't live up to my standards, I did not often offer the grace You offered Your apostles.

Neither do I think of any occasions when You let them run over You. You stood Your ground using healthy boundaries combined with grace and love. Wow! How did You do it? Teach me.

Forgive me, Lord, for all the times I've not set healthy boundaries and for all the times I've not been gracious about folks not living up to the standards I set for them. Be patient with me and keep teaching me that I can learn to be gracious when I'm between the rock and the hard place. Honestly, I'd rather never be there again, but You have warned me that life is not easy, and I will have difficult spots in it. So, help me when I'm there. Thank You.

Bit Off More Than I Could Chew

And being found in appearance as a man, he humbled himself by becoming obedient to death—even death on a cross.

—Philippians 2:8 (New International Version)

Suggested reading: John 12:23–27

I've started lots of things that I have quit midway. Bit off more than I could chew. But You, Jesus, stuck with Your task—born as a human, served as a loyal son and rabbi, then suffered through abuse until they nailed You to the cross. I would have quit. Yet I don't think of myself as a quitter.

There are lots of things I complete, Lord. I set goals, and typically I finish them. But every now and then something seems too difficult, and I say that I "bit off more than I could chew" and spit it out.

I'm glad you were not a quitter, Lord Jesus. If You had quit, not only would You not have been glorified (John 12:23), but I would not be following You (John 12:26). Dying was part of Your plan—Your goal—and so was resurrection. Because You finished, even though Your soul was troubled (John 12:27), I have hope. That's what the resurrection is all about.

Lord, when my soul is troubled, I need to lean on You and work my way through the troubled time, just as You did. I think of the time You were in the Garden, away from Your disciples, praying until You had "sweat drops of blood," and I realize that I've never been that troubled. Diagnosis of cancer, divorce, financial woes—nothing in my life has been as difficult as what You went through. You leaned on Your Father, praying, until You had the courage to move forward and tell those men who were looking for You that You were the man they sought. You knew their intent was to kill You, and yet You had the courage, gained by Your time in prayer with God, to move forward.

Remind me, Lord, the next time I have "bit off more than I can chew" and want to spit it out that I need to pray first. I need to rely on You to give me courage to move forward and do what I am supposed to do. Don't let me be a quitter. Nothing I face will be as hard as what You faced. Keep me moving on. Thank You.

Bless Your Heart

The LORD commanded Moses to tell Aaron and his sons to use the following words in blessing the people of Israel:

> May the LORD bless you and take care of you;
> May the LORD be kind and gracious to you;
> May the LORD look on you with
> favor and give you peace.
> And the LORD said, "If they pronounce
> my name as a blessing upon the people
> of Israel, I will bless them."
> —Numbers 6:22–27 (Good News Translation)

You want Your people to be blessed, Lord. You gave Moses words to use as he talked with them and promised that the pronouncement of Your name as a blessing would lead to You blessing. Wow, what a God You are!

So how are You blessing me? As Elizabeth Barrett Browning

said, "Let me count the ways ..." But I can't, Lord. There's too many. But here's a few:

You are blessing me and taking care of me, as verse 24 indicates. How? I have a roof over my head, clothes to wear, shoes on my feet, a bed to sleep in, food in my belly, decent health thanks to Your use of modern medicine and the time in which I live. You are taking care of me. My worries are minor. *Lord, bless the people on the streets with no roof over their head, unsure of where their next meal is coming from. Bless those whose paychecks have been used wisely and they still don't have the dollars to feed their children. Bless those whose paychecks were used unwisely as You see fit and lead them to better choices this week. Bless those who don't have good health insurance and who need medical help. Show them the next steps they need to take to get the medical, dental, vision, hearing, and mental health care they need.*

You are blessing me with your grace and kindness (verse 25). Oh, what a blessing it is to have salvation through Your grace. You have blessed me with a knowledge of You since childhood. As I have matured, You have blessed me with better knowledge and comprehension of Your grace, of Your desire to forgive me all the failures I've had, of Your open arms welcoming me to return to You any time I run away. Your kindnesses are new every morning as You bring me Your unfailing love (Psalm 143:8). You provide me with my needs, both those I'm aware of and those of which I am not aware. My physical needs are obvious, but my need for friendships and fellowship, social interaction, emotional security, mental health, spiritual teachings, and surprises may not be so evident to me. They are to You, and You take care of them. *Lord, there are people whose needs are not being met, and I know You want to meet them. Would You please use me and others around the world to reach out to them to meet their physical, emotional, mental, and spiritual needs as only You can do and as only You really know. Teach us and use us to be instruments of peace in their lives. Thank You.*

You look on me with favor. You give me peace. Oh, I struggle sometimes. I have wrestling matches with You. When I surrender, I have Your favor, big time. I have Your peace. What more can I ask for? What a blessing it is to know Your peace is always available to me. *Lord of peace, You are patient also. Today, help whoever is struggling to feel the peace that passes human understanding by the surrender of heart and mind to You, and to sense Your peace and compassion, to know You care, to listen as You speak through Your people and through Your word.*

In the name of my Savior Jesus, who showed His blessing to those around Him daily when He walked on earth, and who today shows His favor on each of us, raining on the just and unjust, and letting the sun shine on both. Amen.

Blind Leading
the Blind

Lighten thou mine eyes; and I shall behold the marvels of thy law. (Open thou my eyes; and I shall see the marvels, *or the wonders*, that come forth from thy Law.)
—Psalm 119:18 (Wycliffe Bible)

Therefore some of the Pharisees said, This man is not of God, that keepeth not the sabbath. Other men said, How may a sinful man do these signs. And strife was among them. [Therefore some of the Pharisees said, This man is not of God, for he keepeth not the sabbath. Other men said, How may a man sinner do these signs, *or miracles*? And division was among them.]
—John 9:16 (Wycliffe Bible)

Suggested reading: John 9:1–25

You describe the Pharisees as blind to their own sins, Jesus. They were leading others blinded by their sins and trying to conform them to their ways. Just like us, Lord. We are blind to our sins, trying to lead others, being led by others. Yes, all too often, the blind lead the blind.

The Pharisees didn't like that You had healed a blind man on the Sabbath. They condemned You for "working" on the Sabbath. They said You could not be from God, because You didn't keep the Sabbath their way. They were blind to the fact that the rules they had about the Sabbath were their own rules, not Your rules. They were trying to lead this man who had been blind to see it their way. He refused and said to them, "One thing I know, I was blind but now I see" (John 9:25b).

Lord, show me where I am blind. Am I blind to mistreating people who don't believe like me? Blind to ignoring people from unfamiliar cultures? Blind to ignoring my need for You and preferring to make my own decisions? Blind to how much I'm overeating foods with high sugar? Blind to a spouse's or child's addiction? Blind to the demons of my past? Blind to my constant need for You to be my way-maker? Blind to being led by the blind? Open my eyes, Lord, that I may see. Help me be able to say, "One thing I know, I was blind but now I see" (John 9:25b).

Born with a Silver Spoon in Her Mouth

For who knows a person's thoughts except their own spirit within them? In the same way no one knows the thoughts of God except the Spirit of God. What we have received is not the spirit of the world, but the Spirit who is from God, so that we may understand what God has freely given us. This is what we speak, not in words taught us by human wisdom but in words taught by the Spirit, explaining spiritual realities with Spirit-taught words.

—1 Corinthians 2:11–13 (New International Version)

Suggested reading: Isaiah 9:6, Luke 24:45, John 14:26, John 16:12–15, Romans 8:26, Galatians 5:16–17

When I was a child, Lord, I thought we were poor. But now I don't think we were.

I remember my mom saying that some people functioned as

if they were born with silver spoons in their mouths. It was not a compliment because she was inferring that they were spoiled and acted as if they deserved things without earning them. But, Lord, it seems to me that anyone who knows You has a silver spoon—because when we have You, whether financially poor or wealthy, we have the best of all gifts. You so freely provide us with Your Holy Spirit.

You describe the Holy Spirit as a Comforter in John 14:26. He is a wonderful Counselor, giving us comfort and peace. That's even better than a silver spoon.

Lord, You give us Christ-followers Your Holy Spirit to guide our decisions, to help us think through things we are pondering and unsure about how to manage. When we are studying Your word, Your Holy Spirit opens our minds and helps us to understand the meaning as it applies to us at that stage in life. Later we may study the same passage, and Your Holy Spirit may reveal more to us, knowing we are ready to believe and act.

When our hearts are breaking and our minds so cluttered that we can't think, Your Holy Spirit intercedes and interprets our groans and weaknesses. A normal lifespan on earth will bring many of those times and having the silver spoon of Your Holy Spirit to cry out to You is such a great comfort.

Thank You, Lord, that You also allow Your Holy Spirit to help me resist the temptations that Satan throws at me. When Your Spirit is leading me, I can walk away from the desire to do what I know is not right. That's powerful, God. What a wonderful silver spoon You've given to me.

Thank You, Lord and Savior, for sending Your Holy Spirit to indwell in those who follow You. Whether financially rich or poor, Your Holy Spirit is an amazing gift, providing us with the best silver spoon anyone could hope to have while on this earth.

Bottom Line

He went and proclaimed God's salvation to earlier generations who ended up in the prison of judgment because they wouldn't listen. You know, even though God waited patiently all the days that Noah built his ship, only a few were saved then, eight to be exact—saved from the water by the water. The waters of baptism do that for you, not by washing away dirt from your skin but by presenting you through Jesus' resurrection before God with a clear conscience. Jesus has the last word on everything and everyone, from angels to armies. He's standing right alongside God, and what he says goes.

—1 Peter 3:19–20 (The Message)

Lord and Savior Jesus, where were You for those three days between the cross and the resurrection? Where was Your soul, Your spirit? I know Your body was in the grave. Bottom line, Lord, what does verse 19 mean that You went and proclaimed

God's salvation to earlier generations in the prison of judgment? Were You in hell with them? Were You suffering the pain of the fire that some endure forever? Were You proclaiming the gospel to them? If so, were any saved? Were You protected from the flames of hell? Exactly where were You? Did You suffer in hell for me?

I know You died on the cross, and I know Your body was in the grave, but as the sacrificial lamb, after You suffered that cruel death for me, did You also have to suffer in hell? I don't know, Lord. But I know You love enough that You could have.

For whatever You did, Lord Jesus, I thank You, I worship You, I adore You. I don't need all the answers. I need You. That's my bottom line.

Bucking the System

Now before the Passover Feast, Jesus knew that His hour had come to depart from this world to the Father. Having loved His own who were in the world, He loved them to the end.

Now supper being concluded, the devil had put into the heart of Judas Iscariot, Simon's son, to betray Him. Jesus, knowing that the Father had given all things into His hands and that He came from God and was going to God, rose from supper, laid aside His garments, and took a towel and wrapped Himself. After that, He poured water into a basin and began to wash the disciples' feet and to wipe them with the towel with which He was wrapped.

—John 13:1–5 (Modern English Version)

Suggested reading: John 13:1–20

Lord, it was Passover, one of the most important times of the year for Your disciples, for all the Jewish people. You, Jesus, had bucked the system, and the authorities were angry, plotting to kill You. But You went right on with Your plans, not into hiding like most of us would have done, to avoid being murdered.

You went to the upper room, knowing Judas was in the process of planning Your betrayal. Passover started much like previous years except that no one washed the feet of the guests. So, You did. All twelve of the disciples, Judas included, even though You knew what he was planning. You got down on your knees and cleaned twenty-four filthy feet, knowing they had washed their hands and heads earlier, but their feet had gotten very dirty in the sand and dirt.

That kneeling position made Peter extremely uncomfortable, so he spoke up. The remainder probably felt just as uncomfortable. Lord, we're just as uncomfortable when we think about what You did for us—You died on the cross, the cruelest way to die at that time. You did it for them and for us. A miracle happened three days later—You were resurrected. People saw You. Talked to You. Touched You. Watched You eat.

What did Judas experience, Lord? You knew he was up to no good. How did he go from thinking and planning to actually being paid to betray You? What happened in his mind, heart, soul? How did he feel about You washing his feet? Proud? Ashamed? Angry? Was he in denial of his feelings? Did his desire for his way, for the money, excite him? Was there a hint of guilt starting?

More importantly, when we reject You and Your way, how do we feel? Do we look for rules and hierarchy to defend ourselves, make us feel good about what we are doing? Do we get down on our knees and look up to You, seeking forgiveness? Do we go on with life as if we had the right to reject You and yet believing You have responsibility to forgive us? Do we look for checkboxes to mark off and keep score? Do we buck Your system, try to create our own?

We believe, and we have salvation because of what You did. Help our unbelief that leads to bucking Your system, embracing rules, and looking for a hierarchy to make us feel self-sufficient.

Guide each of us to get down on our knees and look up at You, that we may see You from our knees with simple faith and a desire to obey You. May it be so, dear Jesus, who suffered so severely for each of us.

Burning a Hole in His Pocket

Then he went into Jericho and was making his way through it. And here we find a wealthy man called Zacchaeus, a chief collector of taxes, wanting to see what sort of person Jesus was. But the crowd prevented him from doing so, for he was noticeably short. So he ran ahead and climbed up into a sycamore tree to get a view of Jesus as he was heading that way. When Jesus reached the spot, he looked up and saw the man and said, "Zacchaeus, hurry up and come down. I must be your guest today." So Zacchaeus hurriedly climbed down and gladly welcomed him. But the bystanders muttered their disapproval, saying, "Now he has gone to stay with a real sinner." But Zacchaeus himself stopped and said to the Lord, "Look, sir, I will give half my property to the poor. And if I have swindled anybody out of anything I will pay him back four times as much," Jesus said to him, "Salvation has come to this house today.

Zacchaeus is a descendant of Abraham, and it was the lost the Son of Man came to seek—and to save."

—Luke 19:1–9 (J. B. Phillips New Testament)

You know, Lord, I'm amazed at what I don't know. It just dawned on me that the healing of the blind man in Luke 18 and the story of Zacchaeus were on the same day, and that they probably saw each other as Jesus made His way down the road, may have even known each other. Is that because they were stand-alone stories in Sunday school classes when I was a child?

Mark tells us that the blind man was named Bartimaeus. It's fascinating to think about the possibility of him and Zacchaeus knowing each other. Perhaps Zacchaeus passed by Bartimaeus the beggar on the road, avoiding him to keep from giving him any of the money that he wanted to keep in his own pockets. On the other hand, could Bartimaeus have been one of the people that Zacchaeus took too much money from, making him even poorer than he already was?

What about the day Jesus was walking on the road to Jericho with Bartimaeus among his followers, praising him because he was no longer blind? When Jesus looked into the tree to see Zacchaeus, did Bartimaeus look up also? Did he see a man who had mistreated him? Or were they strangers? Did Zacchaeus give some of the money that was now burning a hole in his pocket to Bartimaeus? Did he invite him to dinner along with Jesus?

Oh, I'm full of questions, Lord, but these are not important things. More important is how I respond. How do I treat beggars? Do I profile them as lazy, as people who abuse the resources they have? How do I treat rich folks? Do I profile them as having no interest in You but content with their self-sufficiency or with selfishly keeping their money in their pockets, not sharing? Is the money I have burning a hole in my pocket to take care of selfish desires I have, or is it burning a hole in my pocket to share with beggars and those with needs? Those are the important questions. My heart needs a checkup so that my pocket change is used wisely. Maybe it is my heart that needs a hole burned in it.

Bursting at the Seams

And all the believers met together constantly
and shared everything with each other, selling
their possessions and dividing with those in need.
They worshiped together regularly at the Temple
each day, met in small groups in homes for
Communion, and shared their meals with great
joy and thankfulness, praising God. The whole
city was favorable to them, and each day God
added to them all who were being saved.

—Acts 2:44–47 (The Living Bible)

S ounds like these folks were bursting at the seams to talk about
You, Jesus. They were excited about You, willing to share,
worshiping You at the temple and in their homes. Wow, they
honestly thought of You as great and mighty. They loved You.

That was in Jerusalem, where there was a temple. But what
about the folks in outlying regions? What were their worship
services like, Lord? Where did they meet? Were they at the
synagogue used the day before for Sabbath services? Were they

still meeting on the Sabbath? Did You care which day they were meeting on, or was Your concern with their hearts, their attitudes? Were they in homes? By the river, under a tree? What did their services, their worship of You, look like? Were they still singing the songs they had sung as non-Christ followers, or had they quickly written songs about You, Jesus?

How did scriptures move them? They didn't have any of Paul's letters yet, didn't know anything from the New Testament except what Peter and John and the other apostles were teaching them. Was the Holy Spirit touching their hearts, opening their minds to better understand that the scriptures recorded on the scrolls had been fulfilled to a considerable extent by the resurrection of Jesus? Did they see history as one story, or did they separate the stories, not seeing the connection?

That church was growing, Lord. Folks were being added every day. For that to happen so rapidly, all of them must have been bursting at the seams to talk about You. Was the temple "bursting at the seams," needing more space for them all to worship? Were they in the Court of the Gentiles, open air, where Jesus had done a lot of teaching? Did they all worship at one time, or did they just gather in small groups with whoever was available, inviting those around them to join in, perhaps?

They must have been talking about You, connecting history to their present day. Is that what we need to be doing? Help us make those connections and share Your story with others so that our hearts are bursting at the seams to share the good news You offer so freely to all.

Busy as a Beaver

After this the Lord appointed seventy-two others and sent them two by two ahead of him to every town and place where he was about to go.

On one occasion an expert in the law stood up to test Jesus. "Teacher," he asked, "what must I do to inherit eternal life?"

"Martha, Martha," the Lord answered, "you are worried and upset about many things, [42] but few things are needed—or indeed only one. Mary has chosen what is better, and it will not be taken away from her."

—Luke 10:1, 25, 41–42 (New International Version)

Suggested reading: Luke 10

What an interesting series of events, Lord. First (Luke 10:1–12) You send out a bunch of Your followers and tell them to heal the sick in the towns they go into. Then You tell the story of the good Samaritan and want the rich young ruler to go and do likewise (Luke 10:13). Next, You go to the home of Mary and Martha and instruct Martha to slow down and listen (Luke 10:38–42). Two of the stories seem to indicate we are to work, but the other says working is not as important as listening to You.

So were the seventy-two that You sent out to gather the harvest, heal the sick, and minister to the people busy as beavers? I'm sure there were enough people in each town to make them terribly busy just healing the sick, but that was not all they had to do. When they came back to You, they reported their successes with excitement. Did they stop to worship and adore You? You remind them that their joy is to be in You and their reward is not in their work accomplishments. How long were they gone? Did they keep the sabbath or sabbaths while they were away?

In the story of the good Samaritan, You are telling the rich young ruler that he needs to be a good neighbor to all types of people, not just those like him. That's lots of work, also, Lord. He could have left You thinking if he did as You suggested, he would be busy as a beaver.

Then there was Martha, who already was as busy as a beaver and very much wanting her sister to also be as busy as a beaver to relieve her of some responsibilities. But this time You say, "Stop. Rest. Listen." This seems like a different message than the first two passages.

A little meditation on it all, Lord, reminds me of your statement in Matthew 11:28: "Come to me, all you who labor and are heavy laden and I will give you rest." It also reminds me of one of the Ten Commandments: "Keep the sabbath." Work like a beaver, relax, get some rest, and take time to listen to You. We burn ourselves out if we don't. We get too tired. We get sick. We need to connect with You, and we need that more than the accomplishments of being busy as a beaver all the time.

I'm often guilty, Lord, of being busy as a beaver, focusing on all the work to be done, and not stopping to rest and listen to You. Thank You for my awareness today of what I need to do. Help me to extend that awareness to each new day ahead.

Butting Heads

I in them and You in me, that they may become perfectly one, so that the world may know that you sent me and loved them even as You loved me.
—John 17:23 (ESV)

I appeal to you, brothers, by the name of our Lord Jesus Christ, that all of you agree, and that there be no divisions among you, but that you be united in the same mind and the same judgment.
1 Corinthians 1:10 (ESV)

Sovereign and Holy Lord, the Almighty God of the New International Version, the Creator of life, the God Who is love, help us live love together. We know that loving our brothers and sisters, our communities, our families is critical to unity. Yet sometimes we like to butt heads. We know in our minds it is foolish, but our emotions don't follow.

Unity is hard. We don't agree completely with others on politics, on religious views, on how to best care for the earth, or even how to care for others. We think our way is best. Often, we argue for what we think is right and best and create gaps in our relationships with other believers in Christ, Who prayed for us to have unity. We need Your forgiveness for the times we have butted heads and thus contributed to division rather than unity, We need You to create a desire in us to feel and be united with fellow Christians, even when we disagree with them on topics like politics, race relationships, on what is sin and what is just a bad habit, on the definitions of important concepts, and the list goes on and on, including silly things we divide over such as the color of the carpet.

Lead us to be aware of our need for unity and the steps we can take to create better unity, to make You the reason we work for unity, and to focus on You and the things we can be united about—including our faith in You.

We love You, Lord. That's one thing we can feel united about. Increase our love. Through Jesus Who prayed for our unity, even after choosing men who butted heads because they had opposite beliefs as part of His twelve apostles, Amen.

Calls Them on the Carpet

But Jesus put it right back on them. "Why do you use your rules to play fast and loose with God's commands? God clearly says, 'Respect your father and mother,' and, 'Anyone denouncing father or mother should be killed.' But you weasel around that by saying, 'Whoever wants to, can say to father and mother, What I owed to you I've given to God.' That can hardly be called respecting a parent. You cancel God's command by your rules. Frauds. Isaiah's prophecy of you hit the bull's-eye:

> These people make a big show
>   of saying the right thing,
>   but their heart isn't in it.
> They act like they're worshiping me,
>   but they don't mean it.
> They just use me as a cover
> for teaching whatever suits their fancy."
>   —Matthew 15:3–9

You're funny, Jesus. I know, You were calling these legalistic people on the carpet and scolding them, but it's funny. I know it was not funny to them, and Your logic and courage put them to shame, and they may have felt a little guilty covered up by their anger. But still, I smile and even laugh as I consider them being so proud of themselves for thinking they had a loophole to catch You, and You turned the tables on them. Yes, You're funny; that is, when I'm not the one You're calling on the carpet.

I need to stop and think about this thing, analyze myself, realize where You could call me a hypocrite, and You would be right. I'm sure not perfect, and I know You could easily catch me.

I take so many of my choices and behaviors for granted. They are normal in our American society, even in the American churches. But I need to look at how I treat people who are different than me—the physically handicapped, people with a different color complexion, people that I judge as being hypochondriacs, people that have different political views than I have. Do I ignore them, walk on the other side of the street to avoid them? Do I pretend they don't exist? Do I speak unkindly to them? Do I criticize them? Do I gossip about them? Am I judging them, jumping to conclusions without even knowing them and their hearts? Am I being hypocritical?

Another thing, Jesus, I like to indulge. Sometimes it's TV, sometimes it's food, sometimes it is reading, sometimes it's something as harmless as a jigsaw puzzle, but it is still indulging, if I am not taking care of the important stuff. I have friends that indulge in things that cause harm to their bodies too—diabetics who eat too much sugar, alcoholics who need to avoid alcohol at all costs but drink it anyway, gamblers who buy lottery tickets with money needed to feed their children. Are we being hypocritical? Would You call us on the carpet if You were physically here with us? It would be in our best interest for You to do so, using other people, or whatever means You choose. We may like our indulgences, but they are not good for us.

What about procrastination, Lord? It is so easy to put off doing things I don't like. But is it wise? Getting all those papers together for taxes is not fun. Not going to the gym or not going for a walk because I would rather veg out on TV or a game—that's procrastination. Reading a novel and avoiding Bible reading is another way I have procrastinated. Yet, in my mind, I am quick to judge others for such behavior … oh, I don't say it aloud, but You know my thoughts.

Bottom line, Lord: I'm a hypocrite too. You could call me on the carpet every day of my life, and You probably should.

Maybe You're not funny, Jesus. Maybe I need to put myself in the shoes of the folks with whom You were talking. This is serious stuff.

Came Through with Flying Colors

With your help I can advance against a troop;
with my God I can scale a wall …
He makes my feet like the feet of a deer;
he causes me to stand on the heights.
He trains my hands for battle;
my arms can bend a bow of bronze.
—Psalm 18:29, 33–34 (New
International Version)

God of the past, the present, the future: You came through for David thousands of years ago, and he wrote this psalm. He shows us how winsome You were with the flying colors he writes about.

Thinking back over the years, repeatedly, You've come through for me, often when I failed, sometimes when I was trying, always when I surrendered. You fixed the messes I created.

Remember that time when I was not sure of how to pay the bills? I saw no way to make ends meet. You came through with flying colors—you got me a second job, just plopped it down in my lap.

Remember that time when I was looking that water moccasin in the eyes? I needed to move, and You gave me the energy and ability to do so—and quickly. You came through with flying colors.

Remember that time I wasn't sure whether to continue a relationship? You slowly but surely gave me the answer. You came through with flying colors.

Remember the time when I questioned whether I was doing the right thing in my decision to move? You gave me confirmation and assurance and have done so ever since. You came through with flying colors.

Remember that time I was not sure if I needed to see a doctor, and You confirmed that I should? You came through with flying colors.

Remember that time I wanted to say something I had no business saying? You didn't let me get a word in edgewise when another person opened her mouth and talked. You sealed my lips, and I didn't make a fool of myself. You came through with flying colors.

I could keep going, Lord. You've come through for me thousands of times. I know from history You will keep doing it. Thank You, God of flying colors.

Can't Get a Word in Edgewise

But the Holy Spirit will come and help you, because the Father will send the Spirit to take my place. The Spirit will teach you everything and will remind you of what I said while I was with you.

—John 14:26 (Contemporary English Version)

Do I talk so much that You can't get a word in edgewise? Am I unaware of Your Holy Spirit, Your answers to prayer, even Your presence, because my mind is racing around, talking to myself? Am I like Job, who spent thirty-seven chapters telling You who You are and how to do things?

For some reason, Lord, this seems to be true in the middle of the night when I wake up and can't sleep. I think about some little something that doesn't really matter a hill of beans, but my mind keeps returning to it. I have the same thoughts over and over. I replay scenes. Sometimes my imagination runs wild, and with each replay, the scene gets worse and worse. I play that foolish game of "what if." You can't get a word in edgewise because my mind is racing at breakneck speed. My emotions lead to high blood pressure as I worry and fret. Sleep is evasive.

So how do You want me to deal with these times? How can I listen for You? You promise Your Holy Spirit to come and help me. But how can You help if You can't get a word in edgewise?

Sometimes I get up and do something to get my mind off whatever it is that is consuming me. But usually just praying what we call the "Lord's prayer" and personalizing it to my situation will do the trick, and I fall back asleep. The next day, I see the situation more clearly and feel Your peace.

If I get up, reading Your word is a good thing for me. You seem to lead me to the right scriptures and speak to me through them, but sometimes I don't let You because my mind keeps racing. Thank You that You keep trying and eventually get a word in edgewise. Your wisdom is so much greater than mine. As my friend says, a still tongue keeps a wise head.

Teach me, Lord, to be quiet and listen for You. Soften my heart so that You can get lots of words in edgewise. You are my source of wisdom and good judgment.

Can't Have Your Cake and Eat It Too

So I have come down to rescue them from the power of the Egyptians and lead them out of Egypt into their own fertile and spacious land. It is a land flowing with milk and honey—the land where the Canaanites, Hittites, Amorites, Perizzites, Hivites, and Jebusites now live.

—Exodus 3:8 (New Living Translation)

Your creation paintbrush was busy with the beautiful butterflies You created, Lord. The same is true with the wide array of flowers. You are so amazing. But we are destroying them, taking away their native habitat because we need it for homes, for businesses, for industry. But we also need bread, vegetables, and fruits. We can't have them without pollinators, so we need native habitat to sustain the pollinators so they can visit farms and pollinate our fruits, vegetables, and grains that the wind doesn't pollinate. We need our cake but want to eat our cake. How can we have both pollinators and have land for buildings? You promised the Israelites a land flowing with milk and honey. That meant they needed pollinators just as we do.

So what do we do? Help us use our creativity with which You created us to figure out ways to plant native wildflowers for the pollinators. Oh, yes, our yards are a good place to start, but only a small percentage of us have yards close to farms and few of us have vegetable gardens or fruit trees. Still every little bit helps.

What about other places that are public land? Could our municipal buildings have native plants and habitat? What about spaces alongside our highways? There are utility companies that have corridors that run across our lands in many states. Could they be used for wildflowers and pollinators? Could farmers plant wildflowers next to their fields to attract more bees and butterflies, create more milk and honey, as well as vegetables, grains, fruits? Lots of states have retention ponds around buildings and along highways. Could they be used to increase our number of pollinators? What about the tops of some of our buildings?

Lord, teach us about the plant diversity and clustering that is needed, and give us the creative ideas to be able to have our cake and eat it too by having both land for our buildings and for our pollinators. Help us to know when to mow and when to let the flowers grow. Thank You.

Can't Put Toothpaste Back in the Tube

Brothers and sisters, in light of all I have shared with you about God's mercies, I urge you to offer your bodies as a living and holy sacrifice to God, a sacred offering that brings Him pleasure; this is your reasonable, essential worship. Do not allow this world to mold you in its own image. Instead, be transformed from the inside out by renewing your mind. As a result, you will be able to discern what God wills and whatever God finds good, pleasing, and complete.

—Romans 12:1–2 (The Voice)

God of all times, the one who never changes but gives Your Holy Spirit to us to help us change, caring God, we come to You today with a desire to honor and glorify You with our lives. We thank You for the Bible and the teachings You have given to us throughout it. But we feel that to truly honor You by living for You, we need to put some toothpaste back in the tube, yet fully knowing that we can't.

Lord, so often as children, we develop ideas that we assume are true, and we live the remainder of our lives making decisions on those things. Sometimes it happens as adults also. For example, our minds acknowledge that knowing scriptures doesn't make us more saved, but many of us came to that conclusion in our youth. We confess that we have not only believed but also functioned as if "knowing more scripture made us more saved." But there's no way to go back to childhood and change the decisions we've made based on that false belief. We can't put the toothpaste back in the tube.

As we come to know You better, we want to change our approach to Bible study and want to know that our minds and hearts can be transformed, and we want to live out the Be-attitudes in our lives so that others may see You. We want to squeeze new toothpaste for others to be able to see that we are reflecting You.

Learning about the church situation at the time Paul wrote letters to them helps us better understand them, Lord. So does understanding the culture. We understand that the letter to the Romans was written to the church after there had been a time of mostly Gentile believers practicing their ideas of what Christianity was because the Jewish people had been exiled from Rome. As the Jewish Christians returned, they wanted the Gentiles to adapt to their ways, but the Gentiles were resistant, being comfortable in the ways they had been doing things. That's a lot like us, Lord. We too are comfortable in the ways we've always done things.

So, Paul gave some instructions to the peoples of the Roman churches: be a living sacrifice. Renew their minds. Look and act differently—be transformed, not conformed to the ways of others. Now, Lord, we know these were written specifically to the people of Rome—both the Jews and the Gentile Christians. But the question we need to ponder is whether this applies to us? Is it a principle for Christ-followers or was it just something for the folks in Rome?

Well, Lord, it sounds like an eternal principle—something for

Christians of all times and places. If it is, then we need to live it out, let Your Holy Spirit work to help us have an attitude change, a willingness to allow our minds to be changed, and a heart replacement with Your heart. That's even better than putting the toothpaste back in the tube.

Thank You, Lord, for giving us reasoning ability that we may think these things through and recognize the difference between an instruction for the folks of the period in which these letters were written and the principles that apply to us today.

Changed His Tune

Hear, LORD, and be merciful to me;
LORD, be my help."
You turned my wailing into dancing;
you removed my sackcloth and
clothed me with joy,
that my heart may sing your
praises and not be silent.
LORD my God, I will praise you forever.
—Psalm 30:10–12 (New International Version)

David knew what it was like to suffer, Lord—physically with hunger as he hid in caves, emotionally as he grieved the loss of his sons, spiritually as he denied his sin. He knew pain of many types. Yet, he pleaded with You, sought Your mercy, and thanked You for turning his cries into dancing and joy. He praised and honored You with his words. His tune changed as he processed his feelings.

Can we do the same, Lord? So many things steal our joy and

our strength. We feel depleted. How do we get our strength back? Can we change our tune and get our joy back? How did David do it?

One of the things I notice in many of the psalms that David wrote, Lord, is that he starts them off with sadness, even depression, and sometimes anger. But he consistently changes over to praise and thanksgiving. Why does he do that? How quickly did he change his tune? They read as if he felt one way when he started writing but changed his tune as he wrote. But did it really happen that rapidly? Or did he write the ending later than he wrote the beginning? Could they have been written months after the occasion so that he had already worked through the issue?

We're all different, Lord, so maybe David could work through it rapidly. That's not how You wired me. I change my tune slowly, and most of my friends seem to change their tunes slowly also. But we do. Our joy may be gone for a season, but as we use our self-discipline to thank You and praise You, our joy begins to return. Like David, we are changed forever by the circumstances that brought on our grief, despair, anger—whatever it was that had us feeling overwhelmed.

Thank You, Lord, for the process of changing our tunes. We all have struggles, trials, difficulties. We also have a choice. We can choose to keep the same tune or change our tune. Make our new tunes be sweet melodies for Your heart, as David's were.

Changing of the Guard

Keep on telling everyone these truths. And warn them before God not to argue about words. Such arguments don't help anyone, and they ruin those who listen to them. Do your best to be the kind of person God will accept and give yourself to him. Be a worker who has no reason to be ashamed of his work, one who applies the true teaching in the right way.

—2 Timothy 2:14–16 (Easy-to-Read Version)

Of these things put them in remembrance, charging them before the Lord that they strive not about words to no profit, but to the subverting of the hearers. Study to shew thyself approved unto God, a workman that needeth not to be ashamed, rightly dividing the word of truth. But shun profane and vain babblings: for they will increase unto more ungodliness.

—2 Timothy 2:14–16 (King James Version)

Words. We do argue about them, Lord. Oh, it is church, so we call it discussion … but it is arguing, many times. We allow others to look to the original language and what the experts in languages have to say about the nuances of the meanings thousands of years back. We decide on what we believe, and we argue to defend it. We sometimes stick with it no matter what—even if someone shows us differently. Isn't that what the Pharisees did? Did they study the words themselves, or did they rely on what they had been told by previous generations? Did they look for Your heart or did they make rules to support rules?

When churches have a "changing of the guard" there are often arguments about things that are changed. There is criticism, reluctance to change even on things that don't matter one iota, and some folks look for things to argue about. A change in music style is traumatic to some, and arguments between members may occur. Is that what You want from us, Lord?

It may be that "the changing of the guard" brings arguments about who the new pulpit speaker should be. Sometimes we are so comfortable with the way one person does something that we get upset if someone changes how things are done—even though it may only be a tradition.

Lord, help the churches who are currently having a "changing of the guard" to look to You in how to deal with change. Keep us from arguing about words, concepts, things that don't matter. Guide our discussions to be done with love and respect, especially respect for You and what You want to see accomplished in our churches. Thank You.

Chewed Up and Spit Out

The governor's soldiers led Jesus into the fortress and brought together the rest of the troops. They stripped off Jesus' clothes and put a scarlet robe on him. They made a crown out of thorn branches and placed it on his head, and they put a stick in his right hand. The soldiers knelt down and pretended to worship him. They made fun of him and shouted, "Hey, you king of the Jews." Then they spit on him. They took the stick from him and beat him on the head with it.

—Matthew 27:27–31 (Contemporary English Version)

Suggested reading: Mark 15:6–21; John 19:2–3

P hysical pain. Emotional pain. Anger. Fear. Rejection. They chewed You up and spit You out. I cannot imagine the cruelty that You endured.

Just trying to imagine those hours You spent, dear Jesus, as You were heading toward the cross is enough to make me cry.

You were slapped by Annas's official; the chief priests and Sanhedrin mocked You, beat You, spit on You, blindfolded You, insulted You. Herod and his soldiers did more of it. They dressed You in an elegant robe as a way of making fun of You, even as bloody as Your body must have been. Pilate's soldiers stripped and flogged You, redressed You in a scarlet robe, struck You, spit on You, mocked You, redressed You again in Your own clothes.

You did all that for me.

Then they led You to the cross, where You did more for me. You let them crucify You. You died, went to the grave, and spent three days suffering for my sins. Yes, they chewed You up, spit You out.

Then the greatest thing in the whole wide world happened. You were resurrected—for me. I have forgiveness and don't have to pay for my own sinful life. The ones who had crucified You felt chewed up and spit out, fearful of what would happen, confused. Yet You made them welcome to Your kingdom if they were willing to follow You. What a Savior.

Come to Jesus Moment

Saul, meanwhile, began to inflict great harm on the Church. He entered house after house, dragging off men and women and sending them to prison.

—Acts 8:3 (New Catholic Bible)

However, the Lord said to him, "Go, for this is the man I have chosen as a vessel to bring my name before the Gentiles and their kings and before the people of Israel.

—Acts 9:15 (New Catholic Bible)

That was quite a "come to Jesus moment" that Paul had, Lord. He had to face the reality that he had been wrong, and that You, Jesus, were really the son of God who had lived as a human on earth and had been resurrected from death. It was a 180-degree turn, often referred to by Bible scholars as repentance.

My friend needs a "come to Jesus" moment, Lord. He drinks

too much, spends his evenings drunk, not available for his wife and family.

His wife needs a "come to Jesus" moment too, Lord. She tries so hard to control him. It doesn't work. She worries herself to sleep many nights, cries herself to sleep other nights.

The man who exhibited road rage at the traffic light yesterday needs a "come to Jesus" moment, from what I could see, Lord. I don't know why he was so angry and shaking his fist at the other driver, shouting, and using bad language. I do know that he overreacted, and that tells me he needs You.

I recall a student who had a great deal of pent-up anger, and I was concerned for what would happen as she matured. What has happened to her? I hope she's had a "come to Jesus moment" and surrendered to You. I understood why she had such anger. Her stepdad had poured boiling water on her and had done many other cruel things to her.

My friend who says, "Just one little bite won't hurt," and then proceeds to eat the entire pie needs a "come to Jesus" moment, Lord. Even going to the hospital with her diabetes attacks doesn't seem to get her to believe that she needs to skip that bite so she can avoid the big mistake. She needs to be honest with herself.

Lord, I need some "come to Jesus" moments too. I let myself get into denial mode and pretend I don't need to change, but that's a lie. I need to be honest, to have the same "come to Jesus" moments I want for others.

Help each of us to be like Paul, to have "come to Jesus" moments that lead us to the truths and ways You want us to live, to spend time studying as he did, and then be leaders in spreading Your gospel. Thank You.

Comparing Apples and Oranges

Now when Eliab his oldest brother heard him speaking to the men, Eliab's anger was kindled against David. "Why have you come down here?" he asked. "So with whom did you leave those few sheep in the wilderness? I know your insolence and the wickedness of your heart. For you've come down here to watch the battle."
—1 Samuel 17:28 (Tree of Life Version)

Suggested reading: 1 Samuel 1:17–36

What was the age span between Eliab and David, Lord? If David was nineteen, as history suggests, then Eliab was possibly in his thirties. Eliab already knew that You had chosen David, not Eliab, to be the next king (chapter 16). Why did he treat David so poorly? Was he jealous? Was he a domineering older brother? Did he have a tendency toward bullying?

You don't tell us, but one thing is sure: he was comparing David's teenage body to the giant, seeing one as an apple and one as an orange. They were of the same species, but that was about it. We don't know, but I picture David as a strong young man but small in comparison to the giant. In a fistfight, he could not win, even with his youth and good health. Eliab appears to have had the same picture in his mind, which he was very willing to speak to David.

David did something good, Lord, something I would not have done as a teenager, might not even do now—he ignored what his brother said. He ignored being insulted. That's hard. He kept his eyes on the goal and his heart followed along. I would have been distracted by the insult and headed back home, angry, wanting to get back at Eliab. Oh, I would have worked through it and eventually forgiven but not quickly. Those insults would have festered in my mind for several days, and I would have had a tough time with the comparison of me as an apple and him as an orange.

Lord, I need help. Oh, I don't want You to test me with this, but I know I need help to learn to focus on You, not me, when I'm insulted, especially when the insult is the result of me trying to do Your will. I need help to not react when people insult me just as David did not react. His eye was on You and what You could do, how You could win the war. Teach me to focus more on You and less on me, as You taught David. Thank You.

Connecting the Dots

Jesus said, "Truly I say to you, there is no one who has left house or brothers or sisters or mother or father or children or farms, for My sake and for the gospel's sake, but that he will receive a hundred times as much now in the present age, houses and brothers and sisters and mothers and children and farms, along with persecutions; and in the age to come, eternal life.

Holy One, Righteous One: What a joy to live love together. We are blessed to be family with our Christian brothers and sisters, to have people for whom we care that extends beyond our biological and adopted families. You have adopted each of us into Your family, and thus we are brothers and sisters, serving one another.

—Mark 10:29–30 (New
American Standard Bible)

A s I've listened to a series of lessons titled "Live Love Together," I have seen the importance of each word and how each word stands alone (Live. Love. Together.), but they also work together as a sentence: Live love together. I gladly embrace this as my theme for the year for I want love to be the centerpiece of my life and want the same for my Christian family.

Thank You for helping connect the dots, for showing me that communion, community, and commission are at the heart of living love together.

With communion, we worship together, and we meet You as we worship together. We leave transformed (Romans 12:1–2). We sense Your Spirit in us as we sing together, as we embrace one another, as we listen, pray, and learn.

As a community, we are family. Mark reminds us in 10:29–30 that following You meant leaving family for many at that time. The same is still true. But, oh, our family is so much larger. Every other Christian is now our family, and we grow close to those with whom we worship. We give support to them, and we get support from them. We see Jesus in them. They see Jesus in us. We come to understand family, to feel in our inner being that it is "we" not "I."

You've given us a commission too, Lord: make disciples. We confess weakness, a need to grow in this area. Our own transformation is important, but it is also important to expand the walls of Your kingdom and share Your love with others. Each of us is a minister of reconciliation, responsible for creating a culture for change. We can each reach out to our community.

Living love together is an adventure. Laying down our personal preferences on the altar is our spiritual act of worship. The dots are connected. We know what we need to do. Help us purpose in our hearts to just do it.

Cream of the Crop

> Do your best to present yourself to God as one approved, a worker who does not need to be ashamed and who correctly handles the word of truth.
>
> —2 Timothy 2:15 (New International Version)

Sovereign and Holy One, You are Righteous, You are Love, You are the One helping us to live love together. You are the cream of the crop. We honor You, lift Your name on high.

This weekend, Lord, churches across the world will come together to worship You, many in vastly diverse ways. But we want them all to be blessed, as You know they need to be blessed. We want them all to be guided, and You know how they need to be guided. We want them all to bring glory and honor to Your Holy name, show that You are the cream of the crop, as You want to be glorified.

Today, we lift to You each visitor who has attended a church service this year and each that will be at the upcoming services. Guide Christians everywhere to be friendly with them, offer to study the Bible with them, and treat them with the love and respect that we would want if we were visiting. Help us not to judge them based on their dress, what they drive or don't drive, how they smell, or other things that don't really matter. Teach us to love them as You love them, and to gently but firmly guide them to understand the gospel message You have made available to us and to them.

We also lift each person who will be involved in the services. Bless the ones who make announcements with the ability to clearly communicate. Empower the worship leaders to lead us to truly worship and honor You. Help us be content with the songs chosen, not worry about whether we know and like them, but instead focusing on how they honor and glorify You.

Those that lead us in prayer and in our remembrance of You with communion need Your help also, Lord. Let Your Holy Spirit speak through them, and let their words penetrate our hearts that we may truly commune with You.

Lord, our speakers need Your Holy Spirit to speak through them also. Use them to teach us to better understand our roles as Christ-followers and to motivate us to fulfill those roles to the absolute best of our abilities. Help them to "rightly divide the word" and teach us as You have shared through Your holy word. Use these speakers to motivate us to work toward the transformations You want in each of us.

As listeners to the lessons, Lord, help each participant to do a self-assessment, to determine where we need to repent and to do so. Prick our hearts with guilt if we need that, and with intent to collaborate with You in the transformation process that we may become a little more like You in this next week.

Our teachers also need Your guidance and blessings, need Your Holy Spirit to speak through them. Bless those in the classes, and expand the numbers of learners, that You may be honored, and we may be blessed as we seek to glorify You.

Lord, bless our services in ways that are "more than we can imagine." Through our Savior Jesus, the cream of the crop, we ask these things with confidence that remarkable things will happen because of our corporate worship time. Amen.

Cup of Cold Water

And whoever gives just a cup of cold water to one of
these little ones because he is a disciple—I assure
you: He will never lose his reward."

—Matthew 10:42 (Holman
Christian Standard Bible)

It was a little thing, Lord. My next-door neighbor offered to
pick up a prescription for me, then brought both it and a pint
of her homemade soup. I was too sick to be hungry, but I forced
myself to eat a few bites. Her love and concern were healing.

It was a little thing, Lord, but my friend came to my hospital
room and brought me some ChapStick and hand lotion. My
parched skin was so thankful for those two little things that it
made my day.

It was a little thing, Lord, but the receptionist at my husband's
doctor's office asked, "How are you doing?" The tears started to
flow. It was a grueling day, and she cared.

It was a little thing, Lord, but my neighbor brought over the
extension ladder and replaced that high-up exterior light bulb for

me. It provided safety and security for me. He wanted me to be safe and wanted the neighborhood to be safe.

It was a little thing, Lord, but my friend's husband called to offer to move the furniture for me. I had already arranged for the movers to come, but it felt good to know that people from church wanted to help me.

It was a little thing, Lord, but another church friend and her husband came and loaded his truck to the max with things to take to the charity shop. It would have taken several trips for me to get all that stuff to them if the anemia would have allowed me to do it.

They said it was a little thing, Lord, but those two guys came and cut down two backyard trees complimentary. It seemed like a massive thing to me, but they said no, it was little. It was such a blessing.

It is a little thing to get the neighbors' mail when I get my own. They think it is a wonderful thing since they can't walk that far.

Little things are cups of cold water. Show me today how to give someone a cup of cold water. Help them feel the joy that You provide and know it is from You.

Diamond in the Rough

Judah the father of Perez and Zerah,
whose mother was Tamar,
Salmon the father of Boaz,
whose mother was Rahab,
Boaz the father of Obed, whose
mother was Ruth,
and Jesse the father of King David.
David was the father of Solomon, whose
mother had been Uriah's wife,
and Jacob the father of Joseph, the husband
of Mary, and Mary was the mother of
Jesus who is called the Messiah.
—Matthew 1:3, 5–6, 14 (New
International Version)

Suggested reading: Matthew 1:1–17

God of Abraham, Jacob, and Isaac, God of Mary and Joseph,
God of the readers and me: thank You for including women

in this list of genealogy. We've been taught that women were not valued in the society at the time of Jesus's birth. We understand that to a limited extent because we see it in Middle Eastern cultures today. We have heard on the news that girls and boys were being separated in schools in Iran, and high school girls not being allowed to go to school. Women who work in government are not being allowed to return to work. They are to stay home. It appears they have no value other than that of bearing children, with male children preferred. We don't like it, but we hear it and get an idea of what females must have experienced in the Roman culture and in Jewish families at the time of Jesus's birth.

But, Lord, You included women in the list of ancestors of Jesus. Five of them. Five significant women, at that. Four of them were not even Jewish. There was prejudice in the society at that time against non-Jewish (Gentile) people and even partial Jewish people (the Samaritans). They may have been diamonds in the rough, but You valued them as diamonds.

That says something to me. It tells me You valued women. If that's true, don't You still value women? After all, You say You never change.

Some women don't feel valued because of the way they are treated by people, including their own families, abusive husbands, others who emotionally batter them. Some don't feel valued because of what they have been taught about their roles. Some don't feel valued because of societal influences. Some have had their voices squashed and not been allowed to use their words to communicate in ways that allowed them to feel heard, valued.

But with You, Lord, women can feel valued. We look at how You treat us, and we know we are valued. Help us understand how much You love us, just as we are, and how willing You are to help us feel valued so that we can be transformed into people more like You.

You are God of women, men, Jews, Gentiles, red and yellow, black, and white. We are precious in Your sight—precious like diamonds are to humans, whether in the rough or all shined up.

Dime a Dozen

Another day, a man stopped Jesus and asked, "Teacher, what good thing must I do to get eternal life?"

Jesus said, "Why do you question me about what's good? God is the One who is good. If you want to enter the life of God, just do what he tells you."

The man asked, "What in particular?"

Jesus said, "Don't murder, don't commit adultery, don't steal, don't lie, honor your father and mother, and love your neighbor as you do yourself."

The young man said, "I've done all that. What's left?"

"If you want to give it all you've got," Jesus replied, "go sell your possessions; give everything to the poor. All your wealth will then be in heaven. Then come follow me."

That was the last thing the young man expected to hear. And so, crestfallen, he walked away. He was holding on tight to a lot of things, and he couldn't bear to let go.
—Matthew 19:16–22 (The Message)

Most American Christians who know Bible stories call this young man "The Rich Young Ruler," Lord. He reminds me of the Pharisees. His kind was a dime a dozen—common. They were also proud and wanted recognition for following the letter of the law.

But You, Jesus, turned his idea of how to have salvation upside down. Legalistically following the laws was not what You valued. You cared about the heart—the motivation for the decisions made. You reminded him that You are good. You told him (and us) that law-keeping is good when it is done because our motivations are pure, and we are keeping the commands because we love You and appreciate all You have done for us. When he wanted that one last thing that he could do to ensure he'd go to heaven when he died, You told him to surrender his stuff to you, and in his case that meant selling it and serving You.

I'm so thankful You were teaching a principle, not giving a command for all people to sell all. If I get what You were doing, You were saying we need to think of our stuff as Yours, realizing that You can take it at any time. We need to allow You to use it and use us. Our hearts need to value You more than our stuff, our prestige, our status.

That's not easy, Lord. But it sure makes a difference. It helps me realize Your grace is sufficient, that I can never be obedient enough. Not one human can ever be perfect, so no one of us can keep the law well enough to get to heaven. Being good is not good enough. You are always better. But when my heart honors You, Your grace makes up for my mistakes.

This reminds me of the song "I Surrender All." I wish I were there, able to surrender all, Lord. Thank You for Your love and grace, covering the remainder of the way for me. They are not a dime a dozen. They are invaluable.

Dip Toe in the Water

Forgive us our debts,
as we also forgive our debtors.
—Matthew 6:12 (World English Bible)

A lot of versions of the Bible today use the phrase "debt" or "debtors," but I think You're talking about more than just financial debts, Jesus. I think You are talking about anything that needs forgiving. I notice in The Message paraphrase that they say, "Keep us forgiven with you and forgiving others. Keep us safe from ourselves and the Devil." It seems to me You are talking about forgiveness of anything, tiny to huge.

But, Jesus, I'd rather just dip my toe in the water when it comes to forgiving others. I'd like You to jump in and forgive me completely, however. Oh, I know, You want me to forgive like You forgive, but I'd prefer to assess the waters first, be sure that the other person is going to accept my forgiveness, maybe hold onto my grudge just a little longer. Why don't You want me to do it that way? It feels a lot more natural, more human.

Oh, You don't want me to act like a human but like You. You

don't want me to do what comes naturally but instead to jump in 100 percent, head to toe. But the water feels cold when I dip my toe in—too cold to jump in with my whole body. But You say do it anyway; after all, You did. You jumped in with your entire body when the waters were frigid with an iceberg, but You warmed up to the idea of forgiving me as soon as You were in those freezing waters of forgiveness. It was a lot worse for You than for me. Your frigid waters involved death on a cross. Mine involves death of my pride, which may be embarrassing but nothing compared to what You suffered.

Lord, forgive me my lack of willingness to jump in with my whole body and my preference for dipping my toe in. Push me in if that is what's needed, so that I can feel the impact of how great it is to forgive totally and completely. Teach me to swim in those chilly waters that bring the warmth of Your supporting arms as I let go of the past and embrace You. Toe dipping just prolongs my misery.

Don't Paint Yourself into a Corner

Jesus knew what they were thinking and asked, "Why are you thinking these things in your hearts? Which is easier: to say, 'Your sins are forgiven,' or to say, 'Get up and walk'? But I want you to know that the Son of Man has authority on earth to forgive sins." So he said to the paralyzed man, "I tell you, get up, take your mat and go home." Immediately he stood up in front of them, took what he had been lying on and went home praising God. Everyone was amazed and gave praise to God. They were filled with awe and said, "We have seen remarkable things today."
—Luke 5:22–26 (New International Version)

Suggested reading: Luke 5:17–26

My friend is paralyzed, Lord—paralyzed by her guilt. She's asked You for forgiveness. She knows You have forgiven her, but she doesn't feel forgiven. She has not forgiven herself.

She's painted herself into a corner where she is paralyzed by guilt and anger. She seemingly can't leave until the paint dries, but when it does, she repaints herself into the same corner. The guilt is piled on deeper.

The man in Luke 5 was paralyzed. He could not get out of bed. His friends brought him to You but couldn't get to You except by opening the roof and lowering him down to You. You told him that his sins were forgiven and to get up and walk. He was instantly freed of his past sins that had him paralyzed. Why can't my friend do the same?

What is she really saying, Lord, when she says she can't forgive herself? Is she saying she knows more than You know? Is she saying that she's unworthy of forgiveness, and she doesn't choose to accept it? Is she saying her opinion about personal forgiveness trumps Your willingness to forgive her? Is she playing God?

Lord, help her walk out of that corner, across the dried paint, with a willingness to accept Your forgiveness so she will no longer feel paralyzed by her guilt. You did it for the man lowered down through the roof, You can do it for her.

What guilt am I lugging around in a paint can, Lord? Am I using it to paint myself into a corner? Am I failing to accept Your forgiveness and refusing to forgive myself? That's not Your way. You want me to forgive myself, learn from my mistakes, not repeat them—and never paint myself into the corner again. Thank You, Holy Spirit, for teaching and guiding me through this process.

Thank You for gradually instructing my friend and helping her allow You to replace guilt with forgiveness. Holy Spirit, please remind her every time she picks up the paint brush to not paint herself into a corner.

Don't Poke the Bear

> Judas Iscariot, one of His disciples (who was plotting to betray Jesus), began to speak.
>
> Judas Iscariot: How could she pour out this vast amount of fine oil? Why didn't she sell it? It is worth nearly a year's wages; the money could have been given to the poor.
>
> This had nothing to do with Judas's desire to help the poor. The truth is he served as the treasurer, and he helped himself to the money from the common pot at every opportunity.
>
> —John 12:4–6 (The Voice)

Hey, Jesus, if John knew that Judas was misusing the money in the treasury, didn't You? Why didn't You stop him? What was going on? You could have poked that bear and gotten lots of action.

In Matthew 18:15, You tell us to talk with our brother or sister who has hurt us. Surely You felt hurt that Judas was stealing from You and the other disciples. You talk about making friends of the people who have offended us—lifetime friends—by talking with them when we feel hurt. But You didn't do that with Judas. So how do I know which to do—ignore or talk? When do I poke the bear and when do I walk away?

Thinking about Judas, it seems he probably knew he was sinning and just didn't care. He would have denied that he was taking money, produce excuses, done whatever he could to make himself look good. He didn't want to be fixed, so he would have fought You with his words. Poking him would have created lots of problems for You and the other disciples.

Thinking about what You said to do in Matthew, the person was willing to listen, so was reasonable, and friendship could result from a conversation that developed understanding. That person wanted to do what was right in Your sight and was willing to admit error and work to correct relationships. He wanted to be gently poked so he could work to make corrections in his life.

But, Lord, I still have trouble figuring out which to do when. I'm confident it is a case-by-case situation. You didn't let people run all over You. You set boundaries. That seems to be true in Your relationships, so I'm thinking that I should do the same. With Judas, You had a mission for the greater good, and part of the greater good You were doing was dying on the cross, not stopping all from sinning. You educated him just as You educated the other eleven. He had choices. He could have chosen to be honest. He knew right from wrong.

You do the same with us. You teach us, through various people and ways. You give us choices. We choose whether to go on with sins of choice, things we are addicted to, when we want to protect our pride, when we want to deny that something is a problem. Like Judas, we know right from wrong.

Lord, please bless me with wisdom to have good discernment,

to know when to poke the bear and when to ignore. But most of all, help me know when I'm sinning and create in me a desire to confront that sin in myself. I can't fix anyone but me, and I'm not good at that, but with Your help, I can change one little bit at a time. Poke me if I need it and help me use discernment in when to poke others.

Don't Throw in the Towel

We must not get tired of doing good. We will receive our harvest of eternal life at the right time. We must not give up. When we have the opportunity to do good to anyone, we should do it. But we should give special attention to those who are in the family of believers.

—Galatians 6:9–10 (Easy-to-Read Version)

Forgive me, Lord. I tend to throw in the towel, give up, after trying to do things on my own. I forget that You can deal with the issue, whatever it is. I don't tell my Christian brothers and sisters, preferring to keep it a secret. I don't give You the opportunity to use my Christian family to support me, to carry my burden with me, thus lightening my load.

You tell us not to give up. You also tell us to do good for our family of believers. That's our local church. Why is it easier for me to be a support to others than to accept support from others? Both are important. I don't need to carry burdens alone. There are people willing to pray, people willing to call me, people willing to give me a ride when needed, people willing to provide food, people willing to do whatever is needed. But I don't want to be a burden to people. Where is the happy medium between being a burden and sharing my personal burdens with my family of believers?

Also, Lord, You tell me to do good for others, especially those in the family of God. How do I know which folks to help? There are so many with needs. Some are major needs. If I prayed for everyone that I know who has a burden and wants to throw in the towel, I'd always be praying ... but then You said to pray without ceasing. I could always be doing something for someone else and not be able to take care of my own issues or my biological family. Where's the happy medium?

Help me find the balance that I need, Lord. Don't let me throw in the towel too soon when I need help from my brothers and sisters. Don't let me throw in the towel and not help them when they need help. Guide me to the right combination of these two.

By the way, Lord, I'm glad You don't throw in the towel and give up on me.

Drop in the Bucket

Jesus, undeterred, went right ahead and gave his charge: "God authorized and commanded me to commission you: Go out and train everyone you meet, far and near, in this way of life, marking them by baptism in the threefold name: Father, Son, and Holy Spirit. Then instruct them in the practice of all I have commanded you. I'll be with you as you do this, day after day after day, right up to the end of the age."

—Matthew 28:18–20 (The Message)

The King James version says "go ye into all the world," Lord. The interpretation in The Message may be a little easier to grasp and do—those we meet, near and far. But that is hard, too. The folks I meet just make up a drop in the bucket when it comes to souls that need to be told about You.

Lord, there are trillions of people in the world. And there are trillions of drops in the ocean. Trying to tell all those folks about

You is like trying to empty the ocean with an eyedropper. How do we do it?

The easiest place to start is with our families, the people we are with, but again that is just a drop in the bucket. With my family, which is not easy either—many I have little if any contact with, so it's hard to be an example much less actually talk with them about You.

What about the people who live near me, around me, the folks I run into when I'm out walking, in the grocery store, at the doctor's office? If they don't know You, they need to. But how do I tell them? Some reject, some scorn, some laugh, but that's only if I try to say something. It's a lot easier to talk about You to those who already know You. Most of the time, I clam up and don't talk about You. That's not even putting one drop in the bucket.

OK, Lord, I need help. Holy Spirit, rescue me when I feel fearful. Give me courage to speak up for You. Help me to surrender to You and to let You be the one leading me in what I say. Prompt others to invite me to share. Help me have the courage of Peter, James, John, and others who shared so freely in the New Testament. Their environment for sharing was more dangerous than mine. Yet they did it.

Lord, help me get at least one drop in the bucket this year.

Drop It like a Hot Potato

Then they called them in and told them they must
not speak or teach anymore in the name of Jesus.
Peter and John said, "If it is right to listen to you
more than to God, you decide about that. For we
must tell what we have seen and heard."
—Acts 4:18–20 (New Life Version)

Interesting how You work, Lord. Here Peter and John were,
before the Sanhedrin, having been told to treat the gospel
like a hot potato and drop it, yet they refused. It didn't matter to
them that their fingers were burning. They had a grasp on truth,
and they were going to share it. They had to tell what they had
seen and heard. They knew You were the hope of salvation for
all people, and they had the desire and drive to share You with
all they met.

When I was young, Lord, I had a lot more courage about
sharing Your gospel. Was that because I was young, or because
society was more accepting of it, or because I had more courage
as a young Christian? How can I get that enthusiasm again? Do

You want me to spread Your word, and if so, how do You want me to share it?

Peter and John questioned the leaders about whether they should do what was right in their sight or in the sight of God. They knew the answer to that was to do what is right in Your sight. They had the courage to do it and they kept speaking up for You, refusing to drop the topic even though it was a hot potato in their society.

Father, empower our ministers, pastors, priests, shepherds— whatever they call themselves—to be like Peter and John, and to speak up in truth, doing what is right in Your sight. Empower Christian elected and appointed officials to speak up for You. What's more, empower me and the reader with the same desire to share You with all our families and friends. Tap us on the shoulder with a reminder that You are not to be dropped like a hot potato, but to be shared with all. Thank You.

Easier Said than Done

What about us, then? We have such a great cloud of witnesses all around us. What we must do is this: we must put aside each heavy weight, and the sin which gets in the way so easily. We must run the race that lies in front of us, and we must run it patiently.

—Hebrews 12:1 (New Testament for Everyone)

We carry some heavy burdens, Lord. It's not easy to lay them down; in fact, it is easier said than done. Yet You tell us in this verse to throw them off, put those weights aside, not be entangled in sins that result all too often from us carrying those burdens.

You well know, Lord, that there have been people in my life who wanted me to lie to cover up for their choices and behaviors. Sometimes I did it. Lord, that was sinful, dysfunctional, and created a tangle that was miserable. (Thank You for forgiving me.) I see it now in others who are married to addicts. It may not always be lying to family and friends but usually involves lying to themselves, excusing their choices. Yet it's easier to go along with what the addict wants now than to fight. It takes a lot of courage and strength to do what is right.

Our world is a mess, Lord. There is so much anger. As I write this, the news is reporting on a mass shooting in which ten people were killed, calling it a hate crime. There's also reports of road rage. There is the man who stabbed his wife, leaving her teetering between life and death. The anger felt by all these folks is a burden. How can they lay it down? It's easier said than done.

You tell us we need to lay it down, to not be tangled up in the mess it creates, and You tell us to then run the race patiently. What does all this mean? Can everyone get rid of their anger?

Yes ... Praises to You, dear God, we can. Each of us can give our burdens to You. Then You carry them for us, just as the Roman soldier carried the cross for You, Jesus. You had to surrender that cross to him. We must surrender our burdens, including all that anger, to You. That is transformation like You had Paul tell us about in Romans 12:1–2. You transform our hearts, change us from the inside out, taking the scowls off our faces and replacing them with smiles of gratitude. We live in the world, so there are troubles. We have Your word and that gives us hope, makes it easier to lay down those burdens because You give us examples of Your will being done in this world. Until we surrender to You, it is easier said than done, but as we surrender to Your will, it becomes easier to do because Your Holy Spirit picks up the heavy load, and we don't have to carry it any longer. That brings rest, peace, joy.

What an awesome God You are, making it as easy to do as to say.

Elephant in the Room

Jesus traveled to Nazareth, the town where he grew up. On the Sabbath day he went to the synagogue as he always did. He stood up to read. The book of Isaiah the prophet was given to him. He opened the book and found the place where this is written:

"The Spirit of the Lord is on me.
He has chosen me to tell good news to the poor.
He sent me to tell prisoners that they are free
and to tell the blind that they can see again.
He sent me to free those who
have been treated badly
and to announce that the time has come
for the Lord to show his kindness."
Jesus closed the book, gave it back to the helper,
and sat down. As everyone in the synagogue
watched him closely, he began to speak to

them. He said, "While you heard me reading
these words just now, they were coming true."
—Luke 4:16–21 (Easy-to-Read Version)

Suggested reading: Luke 4:22–30

Did You feel like there was an elephant in the room, Jesus?
After all, You were deity, and the folks there didn't see it.
What was obvious to You was denied by the audience after just
a few minutes.

Immediately after You read from Isaiah, in verse 22, they were
praising You, but after You gave a little more explanation, they
were driving You out of town, wanting to throw You off a cliff.
As a child would say, "That's not nice."

When You stood to read the scripture, knowing You were the
son of God, and watching the reactions of the people, how did
You feel? You searched for the right passage, unrolling the scroll
to find it. Then You sat down to teach, as was typical of rabbis
at that time. That was a signal that folks were to listen. The
first words out of Your mouth were to let them know that You
were the one Isaiah had written about. Oh, what a privilege they
had in being there, in hearing You tell them You were fulfilling
prophesy. They were amazed and spoke well of You, remembering
You as a child. Thankfully, to our knowledge, they didn't bring
up that they considered You an illegitimate child of Joseph, just
identified him as Your father.

But You kept teaching. You projected what some of them may
have been thinking. You faced the elephant in the room head-on.
You didn't pretend it was not there. They might have reacted
differently had You not faced that elephant, but when You did,
they reacted negatively. They would rather be in denial than face
the elephant in the room.

You got up out of Your seated position as a rabbi, and they ran
You out of town, wanted to throw You off that cliff. They acted

like an angry mob. You outsmarted them—walked right through the crowd and went about Your business.

Lord, help me have the courage and strength to face the elephants in my life, whatever they are—those hidden idols, those addictions, those denials. You are my example, and I want also to be able to walk through the crowd. Thank You.

Every Tom, Dick, and Harry

You were all baptized into Christ, and so you were all clothed with Christ. This means that you are all children of God through faith in Christ Jesus. In Christ, there is no difference between Jew and Greek, slave and free person, male and female. You are all the same in Christ Jesus.

—Galatians 3:26–28 (New Century Version)

Suggested reading: Matthew 16:13–20

Who are the Tom, the Dick, and the Harry of this idiom, Lord? If I meet them, how will they describe themselves?

As I think about a group of young men, I can just imagine them describing themselves by their careers, their hobbies, their families. That's what most of us do, whether male or female. We might also think of our ethnicity, our skin color, and our birth location. It's easy to list our external attributes, our accomplishments, and our family members. We think of these as defining characteristics of who we are.

I recall from Matthew 16, Jesus, when You asked the disciples, "Who do people say that I am?" The disciples answered with names of prophets from the past that people had speculated may have come back to life. Then You asked who the apostles thought You were, and Simon Peter quickly responded that You were the Messiah, God's son.

Those apostles had been with You. They knew You were not just any Tom, Dick, or Harry. You were different. You had a role— Messiah. You had a father—God. Peter used the same things we use to describe You—Your role and Your family name. But, Lord, that description meant so much more than saying You were a preacher whose family name was Harry. That description made You unique in so many ways. Yet, You give us the opportunity to be Your sibling—sons and daughters of God. As such, we are not described by our ethnicity or skin color (neither Jew nor Greek) by our career (neither slave nor free). We are simply described as "one in Christ Jesus."

Dear God, that means I am Your child together with Jesus. I'm not any Tom, Dick, or Harry. I'm special in Your sight.

You're not any Tom, Dick, or Harry either, Lord. You are my Father, my brother, my closest family member. I feel so special when I think of You drawing me close as Your daughter. Thank You for adopting me.

Fell off the Track

> We don't enjoy discipline when we get it. It is
> painful. But later, after we have learned our lesson
> from it, we will enjoy the peace that comes from
> doing what is right.
> —Hebrews 12:11 (Easy-to-Read Version)

Truth be known, Lord, I'm a procrastinator. I get going on
something but fall off the track. It doesn't get finished. I
can't count the times I've fallen off the track when I would plan
to change my eating habits and exercise plans. I procrastinate with
income tax. I put off dusting until I'm ashamed of the dust. I can
go on and on, Lord, with things I've procrastinated, but You know
them all, so I won't recount them to You.

When I procrastinate, though, Lord, I suffer the consequences.
Is that the discipline that You provide for me? When I have not
kept my commitment to an eating plan, I've gained weight that
I didn't want to gain or developed health issues I didn't want to
have. When I've fallen off my exercise track, I've lost muscle and
my osteoporosis has gotten worse. Because I've been aware of the

consequences of not paying income taxes, thankfully I've gotten my rear in gear and not fallen off that track beyond April 15. If I moved my refrigerator today, Lord, the dust behind it would be thick—making my job of cleaning much harder. You are right. I don't enjoy the consequences or the discipline I receive.

You're also right about the peace that discipline brings. I love the peace You give when I get around to doing what I should have done in the first place. I've always had peace about my income tax because I have kept to the required timetables and not fallen off the track. When I finally stuck with my eating plan and lost a few pounds, I had the peace of knowing I was doing what was right and best. I look forward to the next Dexa scan for my bone density, knowing I've exercised appropriately for there to be improvement in my bones.

Yes, You give peace. You let me suffer if that is what I need. Your discipline is hard but essential for my spiritual health. Thank You for loving me enough to discipline me. A life of falling of the track is not a good life. Finishing the job—staying on track—feels good.

Few and Far Between

Nehemiah the governor, along with Ezra the priest and scholar and the Levites who were teaching the people, said to all the people, "This day is holy to GOD, your God. Don't weep and carry on." They said this because all the people were weeping as they heard the words of The Revelation.

—Nehemiah 8:9 (The Message)

There's nothing like the written Word of God for showing you the way to salvation through faith in Christ Jesus. Every part of scripture is God-breathed and useful one way or another—showing us truth, exposing our rebellion, correcting our mistakes, training us to live God's way.

—2 Timothy 3:15–16 (The Message)

Suggested reading: Nehemiah 8:1–12 and 2 Timothy 2:15

S ome of the stories in the Bible, Lord, lead me to tears, because I hurt for the main character usually. This includes Joseph. His story nearly always brings tears to my eyes as I think of how he forgave his family. Your story brings me to tears, too, dear Jesus, as I think of how You suffered, died, and forgave me. How many times have I wept over the Christians in the world not keeping Your word? Few and far between …

The people to whom Ezra and his associates were reading wept for their country, for their failure to keep Your word, to follow You. They showed their genuine grief over the mistakes they and their forefathers had made. Their crying indicated true remorse, a willingness to change their ways. In other words, they repented, individually and collectively. They were ready to change their ways, and their tears showed their commitment. Tears for their country had been few and far between over the years, but they were flowing freely at this time.

There are lots of challenges and problems in our country, Lord. We have a National Day of Prayer each year to pray for our country, and some other countries do the same. Some cry as they think of specific issues for which they feel a deep compassion and commitment, such as the abortion issue or the gun violence issue. Many get behind the politicians with whom they agree and show deep commitment to them and their policies. We may pray for our politician to be elected, which often means "my will be done, not yours." Help us change the order to "Your will be done, not mine."

How many of us read Your word, study it as 2 Timothy 2:15 suggests, and cry over it? When we consider that You breathed it into the writers for us, that it is useful, how do we react? Or do we even consider those things? Do we just take things for granted, so our tears of response are few and far between?

Oh, Lord, we are a mess. We need Your wisdom, Your

guidance, Your transformation—individually and nationally. We need to repent as a nation, cry over our past and present failures and sins; let our tears be many and close together. We need You as the leader in our country. You have blessed us over the decades, and we need the blessing of tears of genuine repentance now. Thank You.

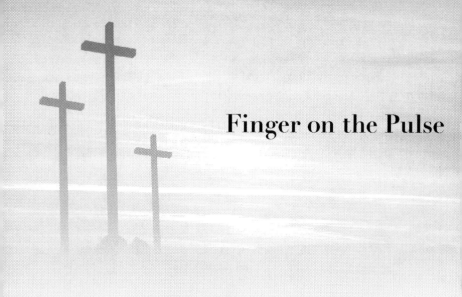

Finger on the Pulse

Now the sons of Eli were worthless scoundrels;
they did not know Yahweh.
     —1 Samuel 2:12 (Lexham English Bible)

Suggested reading: 1 Samuel 2:12–17,
27–36, and Matthew 18:15

Well, God, it doesn't sound like Eli had his finger on the pulse. He seemed to be in denial of his sons' poor choices and ungodly behaviors. Or was it avoidance of the issue? He did finally get around to rebuking them, but they had such bad attitudes that they just ignored him. Logically, I'm guessing that those poor behaviors started years before he talked to them, since they appear to have been young adults when he addressed the issue. It was not long after his rebuke that they went off to war and were killed on the same day.

Avoidance. Denial. I've been a master of them. I've seen family, friends, coworkers, and fellow Christians all avoid and deny. We don't want to deal with an issue, so we don't. You tell us how to deal with relationship issues in Matthew 18:15, but very few people do.

And, Lord, it is true of our own issues, not just relationship issues. We deny that we are overindulgers, saying things like, "God made me this way, so I'll be overweight all my life," or "I got my temper from my dad, and I can't control it." If we deny something, we may avoid dealing with it, as when we procrastinate starting an exercise program.

I don't like having my finger on the pulse of some things, Lord. I feel like if I do, I've got to deal with it, and I don't want to. But when I look at the consequences that poor old Eli had to deal with, I see the benefits of Matthew 18:15 and confronting the issue, whether it be an issue with just me or with another person.

Make me aware, Lord, when I am denying and avoiding, and motivate me to be honest about my choices and to take action to deal with the denial and avoidance. Teach me to avoid procrastination, rather than using procrastination to avoid dealing with issues. Teach me to keep my finger on the pulse.

Fly on the Wall

Now to him who is able to do immeasurably more than all we ask or imagine, according to his power that is at work within us, to him be glory in the church and in Christ Jesus throughout all generations, for ever and ever. Amen.

—Ephesians 3:20–21 (New International Version)

So what was Paul imagining as he wrote to the Ephesians, Lord? In his wildest dreams, did he picture a church building in the United States of America, thousands of miles from where he was? Did he picture missionaries flying from one country to another, sharing the gospel in remote locations? Did he picture church on Zoom during a pandemic that would not allow people to meet together?

Perhaps his imagination saw the temple turning from Judaism to a site for Christians to worship, or maybe You gave him a vision that allowed him to realize it would soon be destroyed. Or perhaps he saw the small-town synagogues becoming centers of worship for Jesus. Maybe he just pictured home churches and groups meeting under trees by the waters of the Jordon.

I wish I had been a fly on the wall of his imagination.

But whatever he imagined, You have done more than he imagined or asked for. You have been glorified through the generations. You have used Christians of many skin colors and locales to share Your word, to do Your kingdom work.

Now, what can we imagine, Lord? We think in terms of numbers of folks in our building, of folks preparing to spend their future with You. We dream of salvation for our families, current and future generations. We imagine transformation of those whose addictions rule them. We hope for bigger and better, but is this what You want us to be dreaming?

May we be like a fly on the wall and see into Your dreams for the church? For us? Help us to trust You as we look to individually be transformed more into Your likeness. Prepare our minds to seek for You to be glorified by whatever comes our way. Your power is at work within us. Amen.

Get to the Root of the Problem

Then they sent some Pharisees and
Herodians to trap him in what he said.
Jesus said to them, "Give to Caesar what is due
to Caesar, and to God what is due to God."
His reply left them completely amazed at him.
—Mark 12:13 and 17 (New Catholic Bible)

Suggested reading: Mark 12:13–27

Jesus, You know how to get to the root of the problem—our hearts, which make us want to be right, to be selfish, to have the focus on ourselves, not You. These guys who were talking to You (in the scripture above) wanted to trap You, so they asked questions designed for that purpose.

We've done that too, Lord. We've asked children questions designed to trap them, hopefully with the purpose of getting the truth out of them, getting them to learn from their mistakes. Trial attorneys do it trying to get either to the truth of the matter or to manipulate the information in favor of their clients. We've done it with our spouses, trying to get our own way, trap them into doing what we want to do.

Sometimes, Lord, we get trapped just like You trapped the Sadducees as they questioned You in Mark 12. You use our words to get to the root of the problem, to help us see ourselves more like You see us. It is then that we grow and become more Christlike.

Today, Lord, help me as I strive to get to the root of the matter—what's in my heart that needs an adjustment. Do I need an attitude change? Or a new heart? Trap me if that is what I need. Thank You.

Give an Arm and a Leg

Then he returned to his disciples and found them sleeping. "Couldn't you men keep watch with me for one hour?" he asked Peter. "Watch and pray so that you will not fall into temptation. The spirit is willing, but the flesh is weak."

He went away a second time and prayed, "My Father, if it is not possible for this cup to be taken away unless I drink it, may your will be done."

When he came back, he again found them sleeping, because their eyes were heavy. So he left them and went away once more and prayed the third time, saying the same thing.

Then he returned to the disciples and said to them, "Are you still sleeping and resting? Look, the hour has come, and the Son of Man is delivered into the hands of sinners. Rise. Let us go. Here comes my betrayer."

—Matthew 26:40–46 (New International Version)

Suggested reading: Matthew 26:36–46

I'll bet You would have given an arm and a leg not to have to go to the cross, Jesus. Even the agonizing You went through trying to accept what was going to happen was horrible. I'd have given an arm and a leg not to have to go through all that.

I've heard the serenity prayer all my life, Lord, but never connected it to the process You went through getting ready to face Judas and Your accusers on the way to the cross. "God, grant me the serenity to accept the things I cannot change, the courage to change the things I can, and the wisdom to know the difference." That's what You were doing: accepting the things You could not change as a human being, using wisdom to guide You through the process of acceptance. You had influence with God, and You knew the plan but to change it would have meant changing the outcome: our forgiveness. You loved enough to go through the process of accepting. Just reading about it, thinking about it, makes me feel as if You gave your heart and soul, not Your arm and leg. That was even worse.

You started by taking Your closest friends with You, hoping they would pray for You. You were sorrowful, troubled, overwhelmed with emotions "to the point of death." I've been sorrowful enough to lie on the floor and beat it, Lord, but not to the "point of death." You were feeling terrible. Those three disciples were exhausted, unaware of how deeply You were experiencing pain. You asked Your Father, God, to take the cup from You, to find another way. You were not ready to accept. It took You some time to process what was happening.

A second time You came back to Peter, James, and John. They

were sleeping, oblivious of what You were experiencing, as You worked through the process of acceptance. You asked them to watch and pray while You went off to continue to work through the process some more by talking with Your Abba God. This time You still asked for the cup to be taken away, but You also added, "Your will be done." You were closer to acceptance as You slowly surrendered to acceptance of the happenings. The guys fell asleep again.

The third time You went off to pray the same thing. I wonder if "Your will be done" was a little more comfortable this time? Perhaps it was, as You accepted what was going to happen to You. When You returned, Peter, James, and John were sleeping again. You woke them and said, "Let's go. My betrayer is here, and I'm ready to give more than my arm and leg for you and all the other sinners in this world. I'll give my life, not just my arm and leg. You are worth it."

Knowing when to accept and when to change are difficult, Lord. In this case, You accepted rather than changing. That was wise but so challenging. Help me to follow in Your footsteps as I work through things I need to accept and things I need to change, whether it be in relationships, in health habits, even in accepting that death is inevitable at some point. My trust is in You.

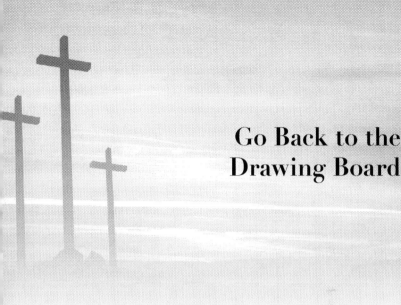

Go Back to the Drawing Board

Pray diligently. Stay alert, with your eyes wide open in gratitude. Don't forget to pray for us, that God will open doors for telling the mystery of Christ, even while I'm locked up in this jail. Pray that every time I open my mouth I'll be able to make Christ plain as day to them.
—Colossians 4:2–4 (The Message)

I need to go back to the drawing board, Lord, and some of my fellow Christians may need to go with me.

When I look at the prayers of the New Testament, I don't find most of the prayer time being spent on the physical needs of others. Instead they are praying for spiritual needs and especially for the salvation of others. They aren't trying to keep the living out of the hospital or out of heaven—they are trying to keep their loved ones out of hell.

Every Bible study group to which I belong has a prayer list of folks with physical needs. Occasionally, someone will ask prayers for a spiritual concern, but we feel we must be so careful that people don't think of the specifics as gossip. We need to precheck our hearts to be sure we are seeking these things for the right reasons, and not to gossip. Our society relishes gossip … we need to go back to the drawing board.

But when I look at what Paul asked his readers to pray about in the passage above, Lord, I don't find him asking for prayers about his jail experience. He's not asking to get out of jail, but that he can share the gospel from jail. He's not listing his physical ailments, his aches and pains, his need to avoid infections or have infections healed after his shipwrecks and beatings. He asks the readers of the letter to pray for him—for open doors, for the gospel to be plain as day. Yep, I need to go back to the drawing board.

Why have we Americans made our physical concerns such a priority, Lord? When I read the prayer requests of the Christians featured in *Voice of the Martyrs*, I don't find them asking for healing but instead asking for families and loved ones, even their enemies, to accept You as Lord and Savior.

Lord, help us go back to the drawing board and restructure our prayers to be less focused on our bodies and more focused on Your Spirit and on getting more folks to heaven. Help us care enough to send our absolute best prayers to You. Thank You.

Going against the Grain

In this all-out match against sin, others have suffered far worse than you, to say nothing of what Jesus went through—all that bloodshed. So don't feel sorry for yourselves. Or have you forgotten how good parents treat children, and that God regards you as his children?

My dear child, don't shrug off God's discipline,
    but don't be crushed by it either.
It's the child he loves that he disciplines;
    the child he embraces, he also corrects.

God is educating you; that's why you must never drop out. He's treating you as dear children. This trouble you're in isn't punishment; it's training, the normal experience of children. Only irresponsible parents leave children to fend for themselves. Would you prefer an irresponsible God? We respect our own parents for training and not spoiling us, so why not embrace God's training so we can truly live? While we were children, our parents did what seemed best to them. But God is doing what is best for us, training us to live God's holy best. At the time, discipline isn't much fun. It always feels like it's going against the grain. Later, of course, it pays off big-time, for it's the well-trained who find themselves mature in their relationship with God.

—Hebrews 12:4–11 (The Message)

L ife is tough, Lord. There's bad news all the time. Bad economy. Family fights and feuds. Cancer, allergies, broken bones, and all health issues. Roofs fall in, buildings collapse. Ridicule by others, even hate crimes. The list goes on and on … What happens in life seems to go against the grain.

It's easy to feel sorry for ourselves when bad things happen, Lord. It reminds me of that time when I pouted because my Dad had scolded and corrected me. Oh, I was just a little thing, maybe three, so it was age and stage appropriate. But now, if I feel sorry for myself when You scold me, it's not age and stage appropriate. I need to do as the author of Hebrews said—don't shrug it off but don't be crushed by it either. You may not have designed the bad things that happen to me, but You use them for my good. Sometimes I think what Satan plans for my ruin, You take and make for my gain. You use his deceptive ways to teach me and help me. It's a part of my training, just like my parents trained me when I was little. There's one big difference—they did what they thought was best. You do what You know is best. They thought, You know. They did the best they could with what they knew at the time. You do what is best with what You know all the time.

I'm so glad You are not irresponsible, Father God. You are

Abba, and You love me, and the discipline and trials I endure are helping me to better mature in my relationship with You. It may feel like it's going against the grain, but it's really going with the grain. You are amazing.

Got Her Panties All in a Wad

On their journey, Jesus came into a village. There was a woman there named Martha, who welcomed him. She had a sister named Mary, who sat at the master's feet and listened to his teaching.

Martha was frantic with all the work in the kitchen.

"Master," she said, coming in to where they were, "don't you care that my sister has left me to do the work all by myself? Tell her to give me a hand."

"Martha, Martha," he replied, "you are fretting and fussing about so many things. Only one thing matters. Mary has chosen the best part, and it's not going to be taken away from her."

—Luke 10:38–42 (New Testament for Everyone)

If this story happened (or when this story happens) in today's world, Lord, we just might say that Martha got her panties all in a wad. She was frustrated, doing all that work without the help of her sister. There was not a grocery store to run to for chips and hummus, so she needed to make them herself. Just serving an appetizer and keeping things simple meant a lot of work. Her personality was more likely to be a full meal, and that made it even more frustrating—lamb, lentils, and fresh vegetables from the garden are time-consuming foods to prepare. Bread from scratch can take hours. No wonder her panties were in a wad.

But You reminded her that the mission was not feeding people physically but feeding people spiritually. The mission was not a seven-course dinner. The mission was to serve healthy spiritual food to those who were present. They in turn would be able to go home and serve healthy spiritual food to their own families and friends.

You know, Lord, I'm such a Martha. To a degree, that's a good thing. Every group needs servers like Martha. Someone must serve the family, the church, the community group. Every business needs workers like Martha to support and provide for the employees. The list goes on. We need servers. Martha was a good one.

Thankfully, You didn't condemn her for serving. You just reminded her to keep the main thing the main thing—that there was no need to get her panties in a wad. She probably went back in the kitchen and kept serving in her role as hostess. If she didn't, the lamb would have burned, and the lentils would have scorched. Mary may have even voluntarily helped her. You may have too, even though it was not a man's job. You certainly broke plenty of rules with the Samaritan woman, so I can imagine You doing it here too although if You did, I'm surprised Luke didn't record it.

But I'm drifting, Lord. Back on topic, You told Martha to focus on what was important. When she did, her panties ceased to be in a wad, and she felt better. What can I learn from that? To focus on You. When I do, my frustrations are greatly reduced. Then I don't have to be concerned about my panties getting in a wad.

Heard It through the Grapevine

"Father, glorify Your name." Then a voice came from heaven, saying, "I have glorified it, and will glorify it again." The crowd that stood by and heard it said that it had thundered. Others said, "An angel has spoken to Him."

Jesus answered, "This voice came not for My sake, but for your sakes."
—John 12:28–30 (Modern English Version)

S ome said it thundered, but John understood Your words, Father God, or he could not have recorded them. Mark and Matthew also recorded hearing You speak to Jesus. They didn't just hear about it through the grapevine, but they heard You. That's amazing.

Some people today believe You can still be audibly heard at times. Others don't. Unless we've experienced it, we may be skeptical. But we can all hear You by simply reading Your word.

The gospel writers record thirty-eight times, Jesus, that You prayed, talked to Father God. We don't know if all of these were audible, but some were. But the writers don't record Your heavenly Father audibly answering You every time. Three times they mention You hearing the Father's audible words. But the words weren't for the public except in the scripture above. They were for You and John the Baptist once, You and three disciples once, but for the crowd in the scripture above, according to verse 30. Yet You were the one who really understood it.

Thirty-eight times were a drop in the bucket compared to the number of times You talked with the Father, Jesus. I've talked to You a lot more than that. The last few years it's been daily, multiple times a day. I feel like I carry on a conversation with You continually. I suspect You did that longer and more frequently than me. If He only spoke audibly to You three times in Your earthly lifespan, why should I expect to audibly hear Him frequently? I can't.

Yet I think You sensed Your Father talking to You. You knew the scriptures. You felt His presence. You listened for the small whisper. You were tuned in for the Father's voice, not for the grapevine. I need to do the same. I need to listen, to know the scriptures, to be sensitive to Your Holy Spirit taping me on the shoulder, not focused on the grapevine gossip.

Hit the Bull's Eye

Jesus answered, "Isaiah was right about frauds like you, hit the bull's-eye in fact.

—Mark 7:8 (The Message)

Jesus replied, "You bunch of hypocrites. Isaiah the prophet described you very well when he said, 'These people speak very prettily about the Lord, but they have no love for him at all. Their worship is a farce, for they claim that God commands the people to obey their petty rules.' How right Isaiah was. For you ignore God's specific orders and substitute your own traditions."

—Mark 7:6–8 (Living Bible)

Y ou didn't beat around the bush, Lord. You hit the bull's eye when You were talking to the Pharisees, and You let them know exactly what You thought about their hypocritical behavior. I'm glad I wasn't in their shoes—but wait, I am. I'm just as hypocritical. Folks are just as likely to say of me that they don't go to church because it is full of a bunch of hypocrites.

Oh, I try to be more like You, but so many of our human traditions are so common that I don't even stop to think about how they got started or why we think they are so important. For example, Lord, almost every time I "say a blessing for the food," I include a thank You for the "nourishment"—that's probably the only time I ever use that word. I say it routinely, like a robot, without thinking, often not even truly meaning it at the moment, although I truly am thankful for the food You provide. Sometimes I thank You for the "nourishment," and there is extraordinarily little "nourishment" in what I'm eating; I could better thank You for the flavors since it is mostly fat and sugar.

Yep, Lord, You hit the bull's eye. You know folks well. I'm thankful You didn't say we hypocrites can't go to heaven. But You did tell us to change, to determine the better bull's eye to have for target practice.

More later, Lord. I need some target practice now.

Hit the Ground Running

The Master said, "Martha, dear Martha, you're fussing far too much and getting yourself worked up over nothing. One thing only is essential, and Mary has chosen it—it's the main course and won't be taken from her."
—Luke 10:41–42 (The Message)

Oh my gracious, Holy God, I just realized how I hit the ground running this morning. Now I'm exhausted, and I've hardly given a thought to You and Your holiness, Your plans for me this day. I focused on my own plans for the day, fussing about getting things done, getting worked up over the lengthy list of things I want or need to do.

I am so much like Martha, Lord. Right now, I'm tempted to stop and do something else I need to do, but it is not as important as spending time with You. Who knows, if I had given You more than a quick "Good morning" earlier, I might be less stressed. I know from experience that it usually works that way.

How did Mary do it, Lord? How did she sit at Your feet and

learn from You as she also adored You when there was a meal to prepare? She must not have been a Type A. I'm so compelled to do whatever is on that to-do list and ignore You, or just talk with You a little while I'm doing a task, but not spend quality time in Your Holy Word, listening for Your message meant just for me. And now I'm so tired that I don't feel like spending time in Your word, instead wanting to lie back in the recliner and rest, hoping some lunch will fix itself and revive me. All I can think is that Mary must have had a lot of self-control or a completely different personality than me.

This is one of those areas, Lord, where I need transformation. I need You to remind me to spend quality time with You each morning before I hit the ground running. I need motivation to be more of a Mary, less of a Martha. I need to want to change. I need faith that I can. Help my unbelief. Thank You in advance. I'd rather hit the ground running to You.

Hung Out to Dry

The LORD is my shepherd; I shall not want.

He maketh me to lie down in green pastures: he leadeth me beside the still waters.

He restoreth my soul: he leadeth me in the paths of righteousness for his name's sake.

Yes, though I walk through the valley of the shadow of death, I will fear no evil: for thou art with me; thy rod and thy staff they comfort me.

Thou preparest a table before me in the presence of mine enemies: thou anointest my head with oil; my cup runneth over.

Surely goodness and mercy shall follow me all the days of my life: and I will dwell in the house of the LORD forever.

—Psalm 23 (King James Version)

Suggested reading: 2 Samuel 12 and 14

My heart breaks for my friend today, Lord. She feels hung out to dry. I've felt that way, and it is a horrible experience. We don't expect our children to die before us, but sometimes they do.

David must have felt hung out to dry when his first son by Bathsheba died. He mourned for days, begging You to save the child. He was already dealing with his grief over his major mistake in having a man killed, but You had forgiven him. Had he written Psalm 51 yet? Had he forgiven himself? Whether he had or not, he had regrets. He was calling out to You to fix the mess.

My friend begged for her son to live also. You chose for reasons we don't understand to take both David's little boy and my friend's son. If she's typical, regrets are going through her head. "If only I'd done this, if only I'd done that, then maybe he would still be alive." She has called out to You many times to fix the mess. So have her friends and loved ones. But we can't.

Actually, Lord, it may be fixed. You may have fixed it by taking him. That's where we need to trust like David did. After his baby boy died, he got up and ate and went on about life. He realized that the darkness of the valley of the shadow of death was behind and that he needed to move forward. I doubt if it was a quick process. It is rarely quick. It takes time.

David must have felt hung out to dry again when his son Absalom rebelled against him and eventually died. He cried out to You, cried out for his son. His pain was deep, again. He was in a dark valley of death.

Lord, help my friend to say with David, "Surely goodness and mercy shall follow me all the days of my life: and I will dwell in the house of the LORD forever." Guide her through the months ahead when the grief will feel overwhelming, and she is feeling completely hung out to dry, unable to function normally. Bless her as only You can bless—with the peace that is beyond understanding. Thank You.

Icing on the Cake

The very credentials these people are waving around as something special, I'm tearing up and throwing out with the trash—along with everything else I used to take credit for. And why? Because of Christ. Yes, all the things I once thought were so important are gone from my life. Compared to the high privilege of knowing Christ Jesus as my Master, firsthand, everything I once thought I had going for me is insignificant— dog dung. I've dumped it all in the trash so that I could embrace Christ and be embraced by him. I didn't want some petty, inferior brand of righteousness that comes from keeping a list of rules when I could get the robust kind that comes from trusting Christ—*God's* righteousness.

—Philippians 3:7–9 (The Message)

Y ou, Jesus, are the icing on the cakes of life. You make life so much better, sweet even in some of the darkest times.

We humans take pride in our credentials. We work hard to get our high school diplomas, our vocational certifications, our college degrees. Some go for advanced degrees. We take photos at ceremonies and post them on social media. We hang certificates on the walls of offices. We post our license numbers on the sides of our trucks. We mention our trainings in our conversations, describe ourselves with titles such as doctor, plumber, or farmer. We are proud of our achievements, just as Paul was. He had lots of training and was both a tentmaker and an attorney, an expert in Jewish law.

He ceased to value them when he started to follow You, Jesus. Why? He saw them as trash, as nothing compared to knowing You. They had been the icing on his cake but ceased to be as he came to know You better and better, dear sweet Jesus. He suddenly saw the difference in keeping rules and in having a dynamic, healthy relationship with You, letting Your Holy Spirit guide him through life, not a set of rules.

Lord, we train our children to obey rules. That's good, but how can we also train them to follow rules out of love, not as a rule keeper who would gladly break the rules if we wouldn't get in trouble? Help us guide our children to obey You out of their love for You.

Forgive us, Lord, where we are trying to be rule keepers in a legalistic way rather than out of our deep and abiding love for You. Reveal to us when we do this and motivate us to act from hearts full of love for You. Thank You for being the icing on our cake.

In One Ear and out the Other

I said, "God, God-of-Heaven, the great and awesome God, loyal to his covenant and faithful to those who love him and obey his commands: Look at me, listen to me. Pay attention to this prayer of your servant that I'm praying day and night in intercession for your servants, the People of Israel, confessing the sins of the People of Israel. And I'm including myself, I and my ancestors, among those who have sinned against you.

"Well, there they are—your servants, your people whom you so powerfully and impressively redeemed. O Master, listen to me, listen to your servant's prayer—and yes, to all your servants who delight in honoring you—and make me successful today so that I get what I want from the king." I was cupbearer to the king.

—Nehemiah 1:5–6, 10–11 (The Message)

Suggested reading: Nehemiah 1

Nehemiah is one of my favorite Bible characters, Lord. He was so confident in You, knowing without a shadow of a doubt that his conversation with You was heard, not in one ear and out the other. He praised You, pleaded with You, confessed his sins and the sins of all the God-followers in Israel at the time. He pleaded with You, sought Your favor—and got what he wanted because You listened. He revealed his heart to You, and You knew he was serious, that this was a man You could trust to conduct Your will and rebuild Jerusalem.

You know, Lord, I don't always pray like Nehemiah. Oh, I know I don't have to. It's an example, not a pattern for me to follow day in and day out. There are other prayer examples, and some are quite different from this one. Yet, Lord, I like this one, and I'd like to start my prayers with praise more often.

Why do You give us multiple examples of praising You at the beginning of prayers? Even Jesus prayed "Hallowed be Your name." That was praise. Do You need our praise? I don't think so. You are perfect, and that means You are secure. Secure people don't need praise. They like it, of course, but don't need it to feel good about themselves. We were made in Your image, so does that mean You like praise but don't need it to feel good about Yourself? Are You like us in that You like praise but don't need it?

Another question, Lord. When I praise You, does it help me see who I am and who You are? Is that one of the benefits of praising You? Somehow, when I praise You, I realize I'm just a little ant on this earth, and You are big, strong, mighty with control over the entire universe. I don't even do a decent job controlling me, and I sure don't do well when I try to control others. There You are, with control of planets, moons, the sun, and everything on this earth that You created, perhaps even other people on other planets for all we know. Yes, when I praise You, it sure helps me to realize how great You are.

Nehemiah also confessed sins of the people, not just himself. He took a lot of responsibility as he talked with You about the sins of the Israelites. He did not claim that it was only his ancestors, didn't try to blame, but took responsibility for both himself and for them. That was quite a man, Lord. My ancestors were slave owners, and I don't think that was right. Should I be taking more responsibility for that?

Another thing, too. Nehemiah just flat out asked for what he wanted. No beating around the bush for him. He stated that he wanted the king to respond favorably to his request. But he asked, he didn't demand. He told You the result he wanted, but he didn't tell You how to do it. He didn't try to manipulate. He just stated the need and trusted You to fulfill it. I can sure learn from that, Lord. I too often tell You how to fix the mess, and I don't hear an answer. I need to give You creative license to do as You know is best.

Lord, I don't want my prayers to go in one of Your ears and out the other. I want You to comprehend, to listen. Yet I know all too well how often I let what I read in Your word go in one ear and out the other. I need forgiveness and so do my Christian brothers and sisters who do the same. Help us listen and hear, put into practice what we hear. Thank You for comprehending our prayers.

In the Weeds

At this time Dinah, the daughter of Leah and
Jacob, went out to visit the women of the land.
—Genesis 34:1 (New Century Version)

I am hurt and lonely.
Turn to me and show me mercy.
Free me from my troubles.
Help me solve my problems.
Look at my trials and troubles.
Forgive me for all the sins I have done.
I trust you to protect me.
—Psalm 25:16–18 (Easy-to-Read Version)

In the weeds of isolation, loneliness, depression: they have
been common problems during the COVID pandemic, but
they are not recent problems, Father God. You made Eve so
Adam would not be lonely. I suspect Dinah was lonely, wanting
teenage companionship of other girls her own age. David says he
was lonely in Psalm 25:16. After my mother died, my dad was

very lonely, and I've known many other older adults who were exceedingly lonely when all their friends died, their spouses were gone, and sometimes even their children had died.

I've noticed, Lord, that some folks who are experiencing isolation and loneliness seem to hide in the weeds, not let people know what they are struggling with. Is that how it should be? Should they admit how they are feeling and seek support? David did. He asked You for help.

I don't know if Adam asked You for help, but You noticed his situation and provided him with a lifetime friend, Eve. Dinah went off to find her own friends, perhaps using poor judgment in where she went and with whom she spent time. I've seen that happen too, Lord, when teens were lonely and made poor decisions in selecting friends.

Loneliness is real, Lord. Help those isolated to use good judgment, to find friends with whom to talk, and most of all to talk to You. Help them be friends first and foremost with You. Guide them to trust You as David did and work with You to create friendships and relationships that will overcome isolation and depression. Help them overcome the desire to hide in the weeds. Thank You.

Itchy Trigger Finger

When I heard this, I sat down and wept. I mourned for days, fasting, and praying before the God-of-Heaven.

—Nehemiah 1:4 (The Message)

It was the month of Nisan in the twentieth year of Artaxerxes the king. At the hour for serving wine I brought it in and gave it to the king. I had never been hangdog in his presence before, so he asked me, "Why the long face? You're not sick are you? Or are you depressed?"

—Nehemiah 2:1–2 (The Message)

Suggested reading: Nehemiah 1 and 9

Lord, I have two friends who are dealing with depression, just as Nehemiah did. Something triggered it for both them. Nehemiah's was triggered by his despair for his country. One friend's was triggered by her hormones getting all messed ups with pregnancy and birth. The other friend's was triggered by a poor judgment call she made that was followed by some very hurtful comments by fellow Christians. Hormones can be confused in anyone, creating the same scenario. Certainly, we all occasionally make poor judgment calls and have judgmental, harmful things said to us. We are all susceptible to dark days, to depression.

So how did Nehemiah manage his depression? He didn't have an itchy trigger finger. He took time, and he fasted and prayed. The second part of that, prayer, would be good for all of us. With fasting, we might have to fast something other than food if we are like this mom, nursing, but we can find something from which to fast including television or the internet. We have examples in chapters 1 and 9 of the prayers Nehemiah prayed. What can we learn from them as we face depression and dark days?

First, he acknowledged who You are, then asked for You to listen: "let Your ear be attentive" is the phrase in the New International Version. Then he confessed sins, not just of himself, but his country. Now, I'm not sure that's the wisest thing for my friend whose hormones are in a mess. Focusing on the sins of our country just might overwhelm her and make her worse, since her hormones are out of kilter. For my other friend, she could confess that she used poor judgment. Just saying it would probably help her feel better. She would not be praying on behalf of her country, so just confessing her own poor judgment would be a good step.

Next Nehemiah reminded You of Your commitments. That's something each could do. Praying Your promises back to You is always a good thing. It could be praying John 3:16–17 to You, or another of Your promises that would reassure them of Your love.

Nehemiah asked again for You to be attentive. They could both do that. When the king questioned about why he was depressed, he was honest. Each of them could do that also. Nehemiah didn't try to carry the burden alone. He asked for help.

Your word has so many good examples for us, Lord. All we need to do is look, and we find how to deal with so many of our life issues. We can avoid the problems that itchy trigger fingers cause by just following Your examples. You are a great provider for all our needs.

Johnny-on-the-Spot

If we claim that we're free of sin, we're only fooling ourselves. A claim like that is errant nonsense. On the other hand, if we admit our sins—simply come clean about them—he won't let us down; he'll be true to himself. He'll forgive our sins and purge us of all wrongdoing. If we claim that we've never sinned, we out-and-out contradict God— make a liar out of him. A claim like that only shows off our ignorance of God.

—1 John 1:9–10 (The Message)

I like the idea of You being Johnny-the-spot-to-forgive me, Lord. That's good. But I'm not so sure I like the condition: to admit my sins, come clean about them. That puts some responsibility on me. I'd rather You just clean me up without me making any effort.

I'd like to use that errant nonsense You say doesn't work—just claim I'm forgiven, without sins. But You say I need to admit them. So how specific do I need to be? Is it OK to say, "Lord, forgive me of my sins?" I guess not, because that doesn't really help me change, doesn't allow You to transform me. I think that means you want me to say, "Lord, I lied to Susie when I said it didn't matter to me what we did. Honestly, it did matter. I didn't really want to do what she wanted to do, but I didn't want to disappoint her either. Teach me how to be honest and yet maintain good relationships, not allowing people to run over me."

Another thing, Lord, I do sloppy work sometimes. I remember that time my tax records weren't accurate. I forgot to include some things that I should have included. Well, that's not true. I purposefully ignored them. It helped me pay less tax, and I felt like I needed that money. But it was wrong, Lord. I'm glad You made me feel guilty and correct my records, pay the tax I owed. I felt better.

OK, Lord, I get it. I still don't like being honest with You, however. But I understand that You want that of me, and when I am, You are Johnny-on-the-spot to forgive me and work on the transformation process, helping me to become more Christlike. And then You can use me to help others who have done the same things I've done, to teach them. I do like that.

Thank You, Lord God Almighty, for being Johnny-on-the-spot to forgive me when I come clean about my sins.

Keep Your Eye on the Ball

This woman did the only thing she could do for me. She poured perfume on my body. She did this before I die to prepare me for burial.
—Mark 14:8 (International Children's Bible)

Abba, Father, Lord: she did what she could. Her eye was on the ball, and she knew it was important to look to You and to honor You. She didn't take her eyes off the ball, and she scored with You. You were honored and glorified by what she did.

Lord, as my friends and I try to keep our eye on the ball, how can we best honor You? Will You be able to say of us, "They have done what they could?" Those will be beautiful words, Lord.

So what do I have, and what do my friends have that we can use as our focus on the goal of honoring You?

My friend who is aging and preparing for death uses her smile to encourage those around her, pats them on the hands, shares Your love with them. I think You say, "She has done what she can."

During the COVID pandemic, my friend who did not leave

home used her note cards to encourage others. Lord, she still does. I think You say, "Her eye is on the ball—she uses what she has to honor me."

A friend who is a recovering alcoholic, Lord, knows that he can help fellow alcoholics overcome their addictions. He spends lots of time providing one-on-one support as men try to leave their alcoholism behind. He keeps his eye on the ball and helps them recover from years of addictions. I think I hear You saying, "He has done what he can."

Several of my friends are great cooks, Lord. Every time they hear of someone coming home from the hospital or isolating because of illness, fresh homemade food shows up at their doors. I think I see a smile on Your face as You say, "She has done what she can. Her eye is on the ball."

One of my friends, even as she grieves the loss of her son, uses her car, Lord, to honor You. She takes people to the doctor. She takes people to physical therapy. She picks up friends and takes them to church. Her eye is on the ball, and she wants to honor You with her life even amid her grief. I think I hear You say, "She has done what she can."

Lord, I need Your help to keep my eye on the ball, to use what I have, however small, so that I will hear You say, "She has done what she can. She kept her eye on the ball. I am honored." Thank You for showing us what we have and giving us the skills to use what we have.

Leap of Faith

As he went ashore he saw a great throng, and he had compassion on them, because they were like sheep without a shepherd; and he began to teach them many things.

But he answered them, "You give them something to eat." And they said to him, "Shall we go and buy two hundred denarii worth of bread, and give it to them to eat?"
—Mark 6:34, 37 (Revised Standard Version)

Suggested reading: Mark 6:30–44

You took a leap of faith, Jesus, although Your disciples didn't see a way to do so. Your compassion went beyond just instructing people, and You felt their need for food and nourishment.

When You told the apostles to feed the crowd, they probably rolled their eyes or laughed, thinking how ridiculous such an idea was. There were thousands of people, but only five crackers and two sardines. Who could feed five people an adequate meal with that? You were asking them to feed five thousand people, maybe more since the Bible says men, not people.

You took the humble little offering and thanked God for it. Then You broke them up and they kept breaking, not into tiny little pieces, but into adequate food to feed all the people there. Then they picked up more than they had started with—twelve baskets full of leftovers. Now, that's interesting—there were twelve of them, and twelve of those baskets. Did You do that on purpose?

What did those twelve men learn about faith? Were they more willing to take a leap of faith the next time there was a shortage? What do I learn? Am I willing to take a leap of faith? What about compassion? You, Jesus, were willing to take a huge leap of faith to show Your compassion. Am I willing to take a leap of faith when I see a homeless person? Am I compassionate when my friends tell me of their aches and pains? Do I ignore the needs of those around me? Help me to examine my heart and to be better at showing compassion, to be willing to take a leap of faith to help those around me. I trust You to teach me, including admonishing me when I need it. That's how I will learn. You are a fitting example to me, and You are the teacher who will guide me to become compassionate and to take the leaps of faith to grow and become more like You.

Let It Roll off Your Back like Water off a Duck's Back

You're familiar with the old written law, "Love your friend," and its unwritten companion, "Hate your enemy." I'm challenging that. I'm telling you to love your enemies. Let them bring out the best in you, not the worst. When someone gives you a hard time, respond with the supple moves of prayer, for then you are working out of your true selves, your God-created selves. This is what God does. He gives his best—the sun to warm and the rain to nourish—to everyone, regardless: the good and bad, the nice and nasty. If all you do is love the lovable, do you expect a bonus? Anybody can do that. If you simply say hello to those who greet you, do you expect a medal? Any run-of-the-mill sinner does that.

—Matthew 5:43–47 (The Message)

Our world is a mess, Abba Father. Many people don't let things roll off their backs like water off a duck's back. They get angry. Hold that anger. Then get angry about something else. It gets added to their stored-up anger. Finally, their anger explodes. A husband yells at his wife. A school-age child purposely breaks his sister's favorite toy. A businesswoman purposefully cuts someone off with her car. An angry man drives his car into a crowd with the purpose of killing as many as possible. Still another uses explosives to blow up a building and kill as many of the inhabitants as possible.

Anger. Our world is a mess. People are choosing to hate. They are not following Your teaching to love our enemies. They are not praying for the person with whom they disagree.

Lord, we need You. We need Your love. We need the transformation that Your Holy Spirit can bring to us.

But how can we reach the world if we are too afraid to share You? Give us the courage to speak up for You, to share You and Your love with people who are angry. Transform our fear to courage so that we can help others allow You to transform their hate to love. Don't let Your Holy Spirit roll off our backs like water off a duck's back. Don't let those we share the gospel with let the gospel roll off their backs like water off a duck's back.

Lord, answer our pleas for change by changing us. Use us to answer our own pleas.

Letter of the Law

"You are the light that shines for the world to see. You are like a city built on a hill that cannot be hidden. People don't hide a lamp under a bowl. They put it on a lampstand. Then the light shines for everyone in the house. In the same way, you should be a light for other people. Live so that they will see the good things you do and praise your Father in heaven.

—Matthew 5:14–16 (Easy-to-Read Version)

Father God, our country's leaders need Your help. They need ethics that will guide them to live lives that show they want to hit a higher mark than just meeting the letter of the law. They need to live their lives as though they are lights shining for the world to see, providing light for the citizens to follow.

Would You help them go beyond the letter of the law, Lord, so that they do what is right in Your sight, no matter what? Guide them to look beyond what they think is right and to look to You for what is right in Your sight. Help them look beyond the laws written by government leaders at the national and state levels, interpreted by courts, and to look to find what is ethical.

Help us as citizens to hold them to the standards they must maintain to keep the letter of the law, but to also pray so that Your power is available to help them have personal ethics that guide them to make wise decisions for our country. Help all realize what is right in Your sight may not be what we want and help us to want what is right in Your sight more than our own desires.

Lord, to be a light on the hill shining brightly for You, we need individually to have ethics that reflect You. Every citizen needs You. Our government officials need You, whether elected or appointed. Let Your light shine as we strive to go beyond keeping the letter of the law. Thank You.

Like Stirring Up
a Hornet's Nest

The Yi rat Hashem is the beginning of coachman,
and the day's Kedoshim (knowledge of the Holy
One) is binah (understanding).
      —Mishle 9:10 (Orthodox Jewish Bible)

The fear of the LORD is the beginning of wisdom,
and the knowledge of the Holy One is insight.
      —Proverbs 9:10 (Revised Standard Version)

As a child, Lord, I remember my dad bringing an empty hornet's nest home from the woods. He showed it to us and explained that we were never to go near one if the hornets were still living in it. Stirring up a hornet's nest would bring lots of stings and misery.

As I write this, Lord, the United States Supreme Court has stirred up a hornet's nest nationwide. Good people feel strongly about the abortion issue, with some on each side of the fence. Some wonderful Christian people are pro the Court's choice and others are not happy about the choice. Both those who are pro-life and those who are pro-choice believe You support their beliefs. You love all of them. They are Your people.

When a hornet's nest is stirred up at the national level, the news media gets involved. They stir the hornets even more. People take strong stances and get stung by the people who believe differently than them. Often people don't control their tongues and say things that don't show the wisdom they need to use, the wisdom You had Solomon discuss in Proverbs. Social media posts meant to be just a statement often ignite a fire of rage from people who oppose the statement, and arguments follow. People get hurt badly.

Where are You when the hornet's nest is stirred? Right there with both sides. Not just one, but with Your people because of Your love for them, not because of their stance on the issue, whatever it may be. Oh, I know You have standards, but thankfully You don't expect us to all come to the same conclusions on issues instantly. You're just as patient with us as You were with Matthew the Publican and Peter the Zealot, two men with opposite political views.

Thank, You, Abba Father, for loving us no matter what our political beliefs. Thank You for caring about people in the middle of hornet's nests. Thank You for wisdom to get through the tough times and for being our source of feeling loved when the world makes us feel unloved.

Politics have always and will always create stirred-up hornet's nests, Lord. Teach us to love all through the stings and hurt. Our trust is in You for salvation, not in politics.

Making a Mountain out of a Molehill

As a prisoner for the Lord, then, I urge you to live a life worthy of the calling you have received. Be completely humble and gentle; be patient, bearing with one another in love. Make every effort to keep the unity of the Spirit through the bond of peace.

—Ephesians 4:1–3 (New International Version)

Lord God, Holy and Righteous One: You must be heartbroken as You look down at the people You created and see so much division. You tell us to be united, and You make it clear that You want that unity to be in You, in truth. You don't want us to bash others, You don't want us to promote division; You don't want us to make a mountain our of a molehill.

As we read Ephesians 4:1, we learn that we are to live worthy "of the calling." How do we do that? You follow up by telling us to be humble, to deal with each other with love, to be patient with each other, to "bear with one another in love." Does that mean put up with stuff we don't like and do so with love? That's what it sounds like. That's challenging, Lord, especially when adults act like children, wanting their own way, wanting the opposite of what I want.

And by the way, Lord, what "calling" are You talking about? "Live worthy of the calling," Paul says in verse 1. Does that mean that we've been called to follow You and Your way? If so, that means I've got to work on living in unity because that sounds like what You are telling me to do to be worthy.

It gets harder, Lord. In verse 3, Paul says, "make every effort." That means work at it, doesn't it? That means if I'm not having a good relationship with someone, even my spouse or parents, I've got to do something about it, not expect them to fix it my way. I'm not in control of them. That means I've got to collaborate with You on fixing me, not fixing them. That's not easy, Lord. You're asking a lot … oh, I forgot, You gave a lot, as in Your son, Jesus, Who died for me. I guess You have the right to ask a lot of me, even if I don't want to work and just want instant transformation.

Am I tearing the church down? How so? By complacency? Criticism? Wanting my own way? Not listening to others? By willfully continuing in bad choices? Ignoring others? Expecting people to call me but never calling others? Other things? Convict me, Lord, and help me be willing to change, to be the person You would have me to be that Your church can be strengthened through me.

So what am I doing to build up the church? Am I encouraging others? Am I communicating in ways that build others up? Do I talk with people about what a great congregation I attend? Do I compliment the leaders when they do things well? Am I growing, changing to become more like You? Do I love well? Or am I making a mountain out of a molehill?

Teach me, Lord, and show me what I need to do. Tap me on the shoulder, Holy Spirit, and give me a good kick in the seat of my pants if I need it. Help me love my brothers and sisters in Christ well.

You love well, Lord. Teach me and all my brothers and sisters in You to do the same. Thank You for helping me to avoid making a mountain out of a molehill.

Not a Magic Pill

"I have the right to do anything," you say—but
not everything is beneficial. "I have the right
to do anything"—but I will not be mastered by
anything.

—1 Corinthians 6:12 (New
International Version)

Whatever you do, work at it with all your heart,
as working for the Lord, not for human masters,
since you know that you will receive an inheritance
from the Lord as a reward. It is the Lord Christ
you are serving.

—Colossians 3:23–24 (New
International Version)

These are good instructions, Lord, and it seems to me they
may have applications beyond what they are addressing in
scripture. For example, the Corinthians one is in the context of
sexual immorality, but couldn't the same be true of many things

in our lives, such as overeating, overdrinking, and overgambling? The Colossians one is about physical labor, doing our work to honor You, but it seems to me the same would be true about anything we do. Help me think this through.

Lord, You know my friend's doctor wants him to make some dietary adjustments. It feels like the doctor is saying, "Go on a diet; quit depending on magic pills that don't work." However, as Paul says in the first scripture above, we have the right to eat what we want and when we want it. We have the right to take magic pills that don't work if we want to. But we need to ask, "Is it mastering me?" If so, then maybe the doctor is right, and we need to make those dietary adjustments. You don't want us to be mastered by food choices and amounts.

In the next verses, Paul says to work with our hearts, to give it our all. Is the same true about all goals, such as goals to lose five pounds and to stop gambling, or does this apply only to jobs we are doing to make ends meet? If I give my all to whatever goal I'm working toward, then I'm more likely to be successful. Magic pills have never been a permanent cure to weight loss or stopping gambling, so I can't expect them to work for me either.

While we're on this topic, Lord, our society needs Your help with this issue. We want instant cures. We want pills that cure our addictions as quickly and as easily as antibiotics take care of infections. We think we have the right to do what we want to do yet get the results we want, not the consequences of the decisions we make. We don't want to work at it. We need Your help to have a change in attitude so we can "work at it with all our hearts" and quit expecting magic pills to take the place of hard work. You, after all, worked hard setting up the world in six days. You still have work to do with me and with all people I know. You are God of hard work, but I've never known You to hand out magic pills.

Not a Spring Chicken

How can a young man keep his way pure?
By guarding it according to your word.
I seek you with all my heart;
don't let me stray from your mitzvot.
I treasure your word in my heart,
so that I won't sin against you.
Blessed are you, Adonai.
Teach me your laws.
I proclaim with my mouth
all the rulings you have spoken.
I rejoice in the way of your instruction
more than in any kind of wealth.
I will meditate on your precepts
and keep my eyes on your ways.
I will find my delight in your regulations.
I will not forget your word.
—Psalm 119:9–16 (Complete Jewish Bible)

Was David young when he wrote this psalm, Lord? Or was he older, looking back, wishing he had more wisdom in his younger years? Was he a spring chicken or more mature and talking about the spring chickens he knew?

Today, how can I help young people to secure their hearts in You, to meditate on Your precepts, to delight in Your regulations? What about the young men and women who are in jail, or those who disobey the law? Those who are in trouble in school frequently? Lord, would You make Your presence known to them, help them feel Your love? Guide them to Your Holy Word and teach them Your ways.

How about the ones I know? The ones in the youth group at church, my own relatives including nieces and nephews and children of distant cousins all need You. I'm not with them very often to introduce them to You. Would You please put people in their lives who will? Guide their parents to be godly examples to them and to show them that walking with You is better than walking in the ways of the world. That's such a problem in our world today, Lord. Some young people say their parents don't practice what they preach. Therefore, they reject You and Your way. Prick the hearts of their parents, Lord, and help them be more like You.

Teachers are examples to our youth, Lord. Some are good examples, some are not. Help those who are God-loving people to be of more influence on spring chickens than are those who don't walk in Your ways. Make it evident to youth that Your way is the best way, that people who follow You are more joyful naturally than are those who look to ungodly behaviors to make them happy. Help teachers in both public and private schools to be better examples.

Lord, I think of the youth I love. Help me show them Your way. Help them to live for You in their spring chicken years and as they mature and look back on their youthful years. Limit their regrets to things that will help them grow closer to You.

Thank You, sweet Lord.

Off the Charts

Those who accepted his message were baptized, and on that day about three thousand people were added to their number. They devoted themselves to the teaching of the apostles and to the communal fellowship, to the breaking of bread and to prayers.

A sense of awe was felt by all for many wonders and signs were performed by the apostles. All the believers were together and owned everything in common. They would sell their property and possessions and distribute the proceeds to all according to what each one needed. Every day, united in spirit, they would assemble together in the temple. They would break bread in their homes and share their food with joyful and generous hearts as they praised God, and they were regarded with favor by all the people. And day by day the Lord added to those who were being saved.

—Acts 2:41–47 (New Catholic Bible)

The growth was off the charts, Lord. People were believing that Jesus was the son of God, and they were baptized, got together in their homes, shared their food with joyful and generous hearts. They may have put a little more water in the soup to make it go further, but they shared what they had. I can imagine them helping each other as they sheared the sheep, worked in the garden, and wove their fabrics. They were many, thousands, but all they had to say was, "I am a Christ-follower" and suddenly they were welcomed into the homes of other Christ-followers.

They didn't call themselves a church to begin with, from what I can tell. They just met in small groups in homes, by the river, or under a shade tree. Sometimes they may have been in synagogues. They prayed together, talked together, shared resources, and when someone was available to teach them, they listened. They may have sought out people who could read so they could listen to the content of the scrolls and make connections between the prophecies and Jesus. They wanted to know.

They kept growing off the charts. Thousands were being baptized. Where were they baptizing? In the Jordon River? In the Dead Sea? Maybe in the mitzvahs in the larger homes? We know John the Baptist baptized in the Jordon River, but You don't tell us where Peter and John were baptizing at the time of this scripture. For three thousand to be added in one day, it took lots of folks to baptize and a large body of water or lots of locations. I wonder what it felt like to be part of such an exciting movement.

Lord, are You adding three thousand people per day worldwide now? Is Your church growing off the charts? Would You do it locally? How can I help? How do I need to pray?

God of church growth, the people in Acts 2 were awed by Your work. Help us to see You in Your works and be awed for You are awesome, and we lift our hands in praise to You. Amen.

On the Same Page

"And when you come before God, don't turn that into a theatrical production either. All these people making a regular show out of their prayers, hoping for fifteen minutes of fame. Do you think God sits in a box seat?

"Here's what I want you to do: Find a quiet, secluded place so you won't be tempted to role-play before God. Just be there as simply and honestly as you can manage. The focus will shift from you to God, and you will begin to sense his grace."

—Matthew 6:5–6 (The Message)

Abba Father, how do I get on the same page with You? How do I know Your will, what You want of me? How do I come to think like You, walk like You, talk like You? Does verse 6 above really answer these questions?

I get it that You don't want my relationship with You to be a theatrical performance, designed to make others think I'm more focused on You than I am. I don't think this means that it's wrong to stand on a street corner to help others, but if I'm doing it to show off, make others think I'm something I am not, You don't like that. You don't want me to be a hypocrite. Your example is someone standing on the street corner praying loud and long. I think of the man I saw going through Walmart singing "Amazing Grace" at the top of his voice. It appeared to me that he was doing it for attention, not for You.

But Abba Father, that next part—some versions say go into your prayer closet. In the paraphrase above, You say to find a quiet, secluded place. I know there are lots of examples of You going off to the mountain to pray alone, and I know You went to the Garden alone. So do I need to make a weekly trip off someplace by myself? If not, how often? Really, is there a rule or is it a heart issue? Of course, I know the answer to that. Everything is a heart issue. You don't demand me to follow rules. You want me to do things out of my love for You.

So exactly what do You mean by a prayer closet or a secluded place? Are You saying to be alone with You, even if I'm in the middle of people, to seclude myself from the chatter and noise, to focus on You? I know it is best if I can be alone, such as sitting on the porch, or sitting outside, or literally in a closet so that I'm not distracted by things. But You know me, Abba, and You know my mind can wander all over the place, even when I'm alone with You. Teach me to meditate on You when I am alone with You, please.

Another thing about being alone with You is that I can better listen for You and to You. How do I do this? I need Your help to listen to what I read from Your word and hear insights You may give me. I need help to meditate. When alone, I am better prepared to hear Your voice, whether audible or silent. I am better equipped to feel the blessings You provide by desiring this alone time with me. It is amazing that You want to be with me whether I want to be with You or not.

Thank You for listening to me muse, Abba Father. I've concluded I need to show up in my quiet place, every morning, so I can listen to You and get prepared for my day so we can be on the same page. I need to spend time with You so that I can lift the day's activities to You and listen to how You want me to deal with them. I need to relish in our relationship, feel Your presence, know Your comfort. Thank You for being my Abba and my Father, for encouraging me in my quiet place. I love You—and I like being on the same page as You.

Put On Your Thinking Cap

The Father has loved us so much. He loved us so much that we are called children of God. And we really are his children. But the people in the world do not understand that we are God's children, because they have not known him.

—1 John 3:1 (International Children's Bible)

Abba Father, I'm being challenged to put on my thinking cap (which as a Christian is to let Your Holy Spirit guide me). This book I'm reading, *Look to Love,* by J. L. Gerhardt, is challenging me. I've never read the Bible consistently looking for Your love and looking to love You.

I'm like the author. I started reading the Bible as a child because that's what good people did. Then at fourteen, I chose to be baptized because I accepted that Jesus was the son of God and that's what He wanted me to do. With that decision, I decided to read the Bible every day. You and I both know that didn't last. Life got in the way, and that decision was forgotten as teen interests took precedence.

I did still read the Bible when I was preparing for Sunday school classes, especially the ones I started teaching to the preschool children. I had no idea what some of those stories meant. But I followed the script in the teacher's manual and tried to share the story with the little ones. You did teach me some things with those lessons, but I never put on my thinking cap, never asked the Holy Spirit to guide me, and did not realize how much You loved the peoples of that time and how much You love me.

As a teenager, I believed certain things and I would try to prove them to my friends using the Bible. That was foolish. I was reading the Bible not for who You are or for what I could become but as a legalistic believer, much like the Pharisees. Thank You for forgiving me for that attitude.

A few years later, life hit. Hard stuff occurred. I read Psalm 23 for comfort. I read stories and begin to put two and two together, seeing myself more realistically through the stories. My thinking cap was beginning to get results, the Holy Spirit was active in my life, and I started to feel Your love. I was not consistent, however, and I still wasn't clear on what my purpose should be when I read Your word. After reading the Bible using a guided study for several years, I decided that was not for me. It went in one ear and out the other. I was reading it because the church leadership asked me to. Thank You for forgiving me for that too.

Divorce came. Life was hard. I read to seek life, to seek salvation from my legalistic approach. You answered. You gave me hope. You gave me purpose. Thank You.

Finally, Lord, You've brought me to a place of rest, of looking for Your love for me and responding with my love for You. Thank You. I love You because of who You are, not because of what You can do for me, not because of answered prayers, but because You reveal Yourself as the God of love in Your holy scriptures. I can read and look for love. I am Your child as You say in 1 John 3:1, and as Your child, I know I am loved. My thinking cap is on when I read (well, most of the time), and I sometimes ask Your Holy Spirit to lead and guide my conclusions and applications. Help me ask Your help, Holy Spirit, more frequently, and not rely on my thinking cap for love or wisdom.

Returned Fire
with Fire

When He entered the temple, the chief priests and the elders of the people came up to Him as He was teaching, and said, "By what authority are You doing these things? And who gave You this authority?" Jesus answered them, "I also will ask you one question. If you tell Me, I likewise will tell you by what authority I do these things. Where did the baptism of John come from? From heaven or from men?" They reasoned among themselves, saying, "If we say, 'From heaven,' He will say to us, 'Then why did you not believe him?' But if we say, 'From men,' we are afraid of the people, for all hold John as a prophet."[27] So they answered Jesus, "We do not know." Then He said to them, "Neither will I tell you by what authority I do these things."

—Matthew 21:23–27 (Modern English Version)

Those guys were trying to trap You, Jesus. But You saw through them, returning fire with fire. I would have loved to be a fly on the wall listening to You outsmart them, trap them in their own foolishness.

Why were they questioning Your authority? Why did they want Your credentials? Did they feel threatened of their perceived authority? Did they not like Your teachings? Lord, I picture them as proud men, strutting around as if they rule the roost. I picture them not keeping the letter of the law but expecting those around them to. I picture men who didn't feel they had to practice what they preached.

You were smart, Jesus. You didn't answer their questions. Instead You asked them questions they could not answer. That put them on the spot, and they were smart enough to realize it. They knew whatever answer they gave would create a lose-lose for them. So they conceded. That meant You didn't have to give them an answer to their questions.

What can I learn from this, Jesus? It makes me smile to think of how You trapped them, but oh, how I hate it when You trap me. I recall that time I told some folks I liked pleasing people. The next thing I knew, You put Galatians 1:10 under my nose, and I had to realize that I had the wrong attitude about pleasing people. I felt embarrassed. You met me right where I was and helped me change my attitude. You have helped me many times since then when I was habitually trying to please people instead of pleasing You.

You're still smart, Jesus. You know how to use Your Holy Spirit to speak to me and get me to face my shortcomings as a Christian. I hope You will return fire with fire if that is what I need.

Right on the Nose

"If you love me, keep my commands. And I will ask the Father, and he will give you another advocate to help you and be with you forever—the Spirit of truth. The world cannot accept him because it neither sees him nor knows him. But you know him, for he lives with you and will be in you.

—John 14:15–17 (New International Version)

Suggested reading: Acts 4:4–22

After a week to mull it over, Lord, I think the minister was right on the nose: the Holy Spirit in my life is better than Jesus physically with me on this earth. After all, the Holy Spirit is 24/7. In Your body form, as the apostles had You for three years, You could not be 24/7. And look what You did once You were in them 24/7. Wow, what power came through those twelve men, and then what power came through the disciples that followed in their footsteps, both men and women. Yes, I choose the Holy Spirit.

What stories You shared in the book of Acts. It is action-packed, exciting to read and study. In chapter 4, Peter and John were truly filled with the Holy Spirit. Thinking back in the gospels, neither of those guys was bold. As apostles, especially Peter, they could coward away although sometimes Peter was aggressive. Of course, Peter also stuck his foot in his mouth sometimes. But look at what he did in Acts 4—he preached to the people who had crucified You. That took some courage. What's more, they were convinced he was right because about five thousand of them became Christ-followers even before John and Peter started speaking up to the rulers and authorities. They probably knew that Peter and John had gone to prison for teaching them, and they still became Christians. Yep, Your Holy Spirit was working.

What does all this mean for me? It means I can be just as bold, can have a significant impact on those around me. That scares me, however. But it doesn't scare You, and You are the one doing the speaking through me. The power comes from You, and You are right on the nose, every time. I stand in awe.

Right the Ship

Ask, and you will be given what you ask for. Seek, and you will find. Knock, and the door will be opened. For everyone who asks, receives. Anyone who seeks, finds. If only you will knock, the door will open. If a child asks his father for a loaf of bread, will he be given a stone instead? If he asks for fish, will he be given a poisonous snake? Of course not. And if you hard-hearted, sinful men know how to give good gifts to your children, won't your Father in heaven even more certainly give good gifts to those who ask him for them?
—Matthew 7:7–11 (Living Bible)

And even when you do ask you don't get it because your whole aim is wrong—you want only what will give you pleasure.
—James 4:3 (Living Bible)

It's confusing, Lord. You tell us to ask for anything and we'll get it, and then You have James tell us we don't get things because we are selfish, wanting pleasure. What do You mean? How can I right this ship, not feel like I'm hearing two messages and going in two different directions?

Well, Lord, I guess to right this ship, I need to start by looking at both passages "in context"—check the verses before and after them so I know more about what You are teaching in each passage. I also need to think about what the writer was trying to teach the audience to whom he was writing and think about the culture of that time. Since I don't read Greek or Arabic, I can look at Scripture4All.com and study what the original language had to say. Perhaps once I know what it meant to the original readers, I'll have a better idea of what it means today. Oh, Lord, I think it might be wise to look at other scriptures about prayer and see what they say and find what aligns and agrees.

It might be easier, Lord, just to go read what commentators have to say and to trust them, but I'm not sure if that qualifies for studying to show myself approved (2 Timothy 2:15).

OK, Lord, I'm ready to right this ship. You've said to "ask, knock, seek"—in other words, You want me to pray fervently, passionately, persistently, with faith—but not to look to You as "Santa Claus" who provides for my desires that are selfish, that come from greed and a desire to have the easy life. You want me to examine my heart so that I'm seeking to please and honor You, not myself. When I pray in ways that glorify and honor You, it's not just asking, knocking, and seeking—it's praising, thanking, honoring as a part of my communication with You, not looking to You to get what I want. Prayer is like talking with a spouse—it needs to include all aspects of communication, not just asking. It's a conversation, and the listening aspect includes some time reading and meditating on Your word so that I know more about this topic of prayer than when I started.

OK, Lord, help me keep this ship sailing toward the right destination. Thank You for collaborating with me as I question Your word.

Ruffled Feathers

Therefore, I urge you, brothers, and sisters, in view of God's mercy, to offer your bodies as a living sacrifice, holy and pleasing to God—this is your true and proper worship. Do not conform to the pattern of this world but be transformed by the renewing of your mind. Then you will be able to test and approve what God's will is—his good, pleasing, and perfect will.

—Romans 12:1–2 (New International Version)

So I beg you, brothers and sisters, because of the great mercy God has shown us, offer your lives as a living sacrifice to him—an offering that is only for God and pleasing to him. Considering what he has done, it is only right that you should worship him in this way. Don't change yourselves to be like the people of this world, but let God change you inside with a new way of thinking. Then you will be able to understand and accept what God wants for you. You will be able to know what is good and pleasing to him and what is perfect.

—Romans 12:1–2 (Easy-to-Read Version)

Sacrifice: surrender of something for the sake of something else; giving up something one wants to keep.

Transform: to make a thorough, dramatic change in character; to convert; to change in composition or structure.

Renew: recharge, re-create, repair, regenerate; to make like new.

Lord, does this mean You want me to take the things I believe, examine them for truth, and change my mind so that it is transformed, and I change to become more Christlike? Do You want me to give You the beliefs that I hold sacred? Surrender to You and Your will?

That's hard, Lord—"ruffling my feathers." Change does not come easy. I must examine what I believe and figure out whether it is true. If it is not, I must quit believing it, and that ruffles my feathers too. I've lived believing it all my life, and now You are asking me to quit believing it—and not just to quit believing it but to quit living like I believe it. Then You ask me to demonstrate my love for You by laying it on the altar in sacrifice and changing my character. My feathers are really ruffled now, Lord. How can I do all that?

I only see one way I can do this, Lord: by the help of Your Holy Spirit. I need Your help to get these feathers to lay down smoothly, to help me react to my need, to have a new belief and give You the old one as my sacrifice.

Thank You, Holy Spirit, and thank You, Jesus, for sending Your Holy Spirit so that I can change. We'll get these ruffled feathers nice and smooth soon.

Save His Hide

All this time Peter was sitting outside in the courtyard, and a maidservant came up to him and said, "Weren't you with Jesus, the man from Galilee?" But he denied it before them all, saying "I don't know what you're talking about." Then when he had gone out into the porch, another maid caught sight of him and said to those who were there, "This man was with Jesus of Nazareth." And again he denied it with an oath—"I don't know the man." A few minutes later those who were standing about came up to Peter and said to him, "You certainly are one of them, you know; it's obvious from your accent." At that he began to curse and swear—"I tell you I don't know the man." Immediately the cock crew, and the words of Jesus came back into Peter's mind—"Before the cock crows you will disown me three times." And he went outside and wept bitterly.

—Matthew 26:69–75
(J. B. Phillips New Testament)

S ounds like Peter wanted to save his own hide, Lord. He knew how cruel those folks could be, and he didn't want his skin beaten to a pulp. But did he have to lie and say he never knew You? Of course, he knew You. Just a few days before he had declared You to be the Son of God. You had shared with him that he would be spreading the gospel because he understood and grasps who You were.

So, what would I have done if I had been in the courtyard, observing what was going on, wanting to be a fly on the wall, not wanting attention on me? I understand Peter. I am not sure I could have even done as well as he did if I'm honest. I'm not sure I would have had the courage to go into the courtyard to observe them questioning You. And surely when they started spitting in Your face and hitting You with their fists, I would have run for the nearest exit to escape. I hate seeing people be cruel. I would have run out and cried like a baby. At least he stayed and was able to be a witness to what happened.

Well, he stayed until the rooster crowed. That's when he left to cry. He remembered Your words, and the tears of remorse flowed freely. That took courage, Lord. He was being honest with himself, realizing what he had done, repenting. We know he changed and went the other direction, fully embracing You and Your way, teaching others and working to establish Your church throughout the region. He was even strong enough to face the death penalty—one almost as bad as the one You faced, dying upside down on a cross.

Peter. I aspire to be more like him and his good qualities: one whose fear led to lying, which led to remorse, which led to repentance, which led to true submission to You and Your will. What a man he was even if he started off trying to save his own hide.

Scratches an Itch

The Jews established and adopted *it* for themselves and for their offspring, and for all who joined them. They did not neglect *to observe* these two days every year as it was written and appointed to them. These days *are* to be remembered and *are* to be kept in every generation, and in family, province, and city; and these days of Purim are not *to be* neglected among the Jews, and their memory shall not come to an end among their offspring.
—Esther 9:27–28 (Lexham English Bible)

Suggested reading: Leviticus 23

Celebrations scratch an itch for us, Lord. We need them. You established them in Leviticus 23 because You knew people needed them to keep historical events from being forgotten and buried. We've continued to create them because we don't want to forget certain events in history. Every culture has their own.

Our Jewish friends still celebrate the one, Purim, they created thousands of years ago in the scripture above. That's so cool.

They do help us remember, Lord. Our American Independence Day (Fourth of July) helps us recall what happened to our ancestors. Martin Luther King Day reminds us of how difficult it is for freedom to progress. Christmas and Easter remind us of the time in history when You were on earth and the gifts You gave us, especially Your grace and love.

Other countries have Independence Days also. Most nations celebrate the Jewish and Christian holidays, depending on their faith. Other religions have celebrations also, based on their history. Cultural holidays are also common.

Yes, You created man with a need to remember and a need to celebrate. You knew we needed it, that it scratches an itch that we each have. When You were on earth, Jesus, You celebrated the Jewish holidays including Passover. Then You established a new one: Communion also known as the Lord's Supper. We wanted to remember more so we added Christmas and Easter. Our itch to remember needed more scratching.

Thank You for the itch, thank You for the various holidays and celebrations that allow us to scratch. Thank You for our ancestors who did so much for us. Thank You, dear Jesus, for what You did for us individually and collectively. Your love scratches an itch also.

Seeing Things in a Different Light

Be prepared. You're up against far more than you can handle on your own. Take all the help you can get, every weapon God has issued, so that when it's all over but the shouting you'll still be on your feet. Truth, righteousness, peace, faith, and salvation are more than words. Learn how to apply them. You'll need them throughout your life. God's Word is an indispensable weapon. In the same way, prayer is essential in this ongoing warfare. Pray hard and long. Pray for your brothers and sisters. Keep your eyes open. Keep each other's spirits up so that no one falls behind or drops out.

And don't forget to pray for me. Pray that I'll know what to say and have the courage to say it at the right time, telling the mystery to one and all, the Message that I, jailbird preacher that I am, am responsible for getting out.

   —Ephesians 6:18–20 (The Message)

Dear God, I don't know anything about Mr. E. M. Bounds, but I like what he said: "No learning can make up for the failure to pray. No earnestness, no diligence, no study, no gifts will supply its lack." If he's right, that is part of the reason Your apostles asked You to teach them to pray. Without prayer, we see things in a different light. Your light is perfect, and You see perfectly so You can lead us down the various paths of life with accuracy and certainty. Amazing.

When I look at what Paul instructed, Lord, I am even more amazed. "Pray hard and long. Pray for your brothers and sisters. Keep your eyes open. Keep each other's spirits up so that no one falls behind or drops out." That shows the importance of prayer too. Not just praying for myself, but also praying for others—and he even says for us to keep our eyes open. That way, we won't be looking with a different light than You use. And what about that part about keeping others' spirits up? How should I pray for this, and for whom? Depressed people need their spirits restored. Our armed services men and women need their spirits maintained at healthy levels. Our church leaders need their spirits and motivation to be at levels where they can share it and guide others to feel ready to share also. The list goes on, Lord. But honestly, I've never prayed this way. Guess I've got some work to do.

Paul even asked for prayers for himself, and he needed them since he was in that nasty jail. But he didn't seem to be as concerned about his circumstances as he was with sharing the gospel. What can I learn from this, and how do I need to change my prayers?

Continue to teach me to pray, Lord, to talk with You about any and everything, to look at things with Your light shining directly on them. Thank You.

Sight for Sore Eyes

The next day, when the large crowd that had come to the festival heard that Jesus was coming to Jerusalem, they took palm branches and went out to meet Him. They kept shouting: "Hosanna. He who comes in the name of the Lord is the blessed One—the King of Israel."

Jesus found a young donkey and sat on it, just as it is written: "Fear no more, Daughter Zion. Look, your King is coming, sitting on a donkey's colt."
—John 12:12–16 (Holman Christian Standard Bible)

Not long before the Triumphant Entry (as we call Your trip into Jerusalem), Mary had anointed Your feet with the expensive essential oil nard. There was also Bartimaeus who had praised You, and Zacchaeus came down out of a tree to take You to dinner and to honor You as his special guest. In the scripture above, You've left Bethany and are on Your way into Jerusalem for the Passover. People from over the countryside are on the road also, trying to get to Jerusalem when they see You. To them, You must have been a sight for sore eyes. They had heard of You and Your miracles. Some of them may have had fish and bread on the mountainside, multiplied from the sardines and crackers of a little boy. They were looking for a king who would rescue them from the tight reign of Rome, provide them with more freedom, less taxes, and a better life. And they worshiped You, just as Mary had with her nard, Bartimaeus had with his praise, and Zacchaeus had with his honor of You at the head of his table.

Perhaps the praise was a good sight for Your sore eyes too, anticipating what was coming when You got to Jerusalem. You resolutely marched on. I'm so glad those people made Your trip a little more pleasant, showing their love and respect to You. What would I have done? Would I have been a sceptic and held back? Would I have whooped and shouted Your praise? Would I have even perceived that a king was riding a donkey? Those things don't really matter now, Lord. I recognize You when I read about You, but do I notice when Your Holy Spirit is working in me and in those around me? Do I praise You, honor You? Or do I hold back my praises, forget to even think about them?

You are worthy, so remind me to praise You extravagantly, as Mary did. You are a sight for my sore eyes, and I hope that my praise of You can be a sight for Your sore eyes.

Snake in the Grass

So the people shouted, and the trumpets sounded. When they heard the blast of the trumpet, the people gave a great shout, and the wall collapsed. The people advanced into the city, each man straight ahead, and they captured the city.

—Joshua 6:20 Holman Christian Standard Bible (HCSB)

Suggested reading: Joshua 6:15–27

Oh, Abba, it sounds like the Israelites were a snake in the grass to the folks living in Jericho. But You were ruling over the situation, and You knew what it would take to make that wall fall. You were sovereign, in control, all knowing.

If I'd been living in the city and saw/heard the Israelites walking around the city blowing trumpets for six days, I'd have been making fun of them, wondering what they were doing. Did those folks know that the Israelites wanted to take over their city? They had heard rumors because back when the spies were there, they planned to get rid of them, but Rahab protected them. They must have felt very secure with the walls around them. I can only imagine how silly it looked to folks that an army had approached and were only walking and blowing trumpets.

But, oh, You had a different plan. You must have known the weak spots in the wall, or maybe You just worked a miracle. You did many other times, and You still do, so why do I doubt? That seventh day, they marched, and as we sing with children, "the walls came tumbling down." The people inside those walls were totally surprised, just as we are when a house or apartment building comes tumbling down. Unexpected and totally upsetting. But the folks inside those walls weren't godly, had no interest in You, and rejected You and Your ways. You knew they were not helping to promote Your way and were instead promoting the ways of Satan. They were cruel, they may have had leaders like Hitler, Stalin, or Osama Bin Laden or other historical figures who wanted to rule the world, or at least the world around them. Whatever the circumstances, You wanted change, and You wanted people to honor You. So, You allowed that wall to come tumbling down. That snake in the grass outside the city proved to be a powerful force with which to deal.

You still are a powerful source with which to deal. It's rare if ever that I think of You working like a snake in the grass, but You could, and if You do, that's OK. You usually nudge me with Your Holy Spirit, reminding me of things that You want me to learn or do. You use people around me (You did that at Jericho too).

Your ways are not my ways, and I don't always understand. But I know this: Those Israelites' faith must have been strengthened that day to see the miracle You worked. But, oh, I forgot, at least one of them didn't do what You said … but that's another story, for a different prayer.

Thank You, Lord, for Your miracles, Your way of work that is not like mine at all. It's better, by far.

Snug as a Bug in a Rug

Jesus said, "Bring them here." Then he had the people sit on the grass. He took the five loaves and two fish, lifted his face to heaven in prayer, blessed, broke, and gave the bread to the disciples. The disciples then gave the food to the congregation. They all ate their fill. They gathered twelve baskets of leftovers. About five thousand were fed.

—Matthew 14:19–21 (The Message)

Suggested reading: Matthew 14:1–21

Note: many versions say, "five thousand men besides women and children."

I bet those folks felt as snug as a bug in a rug, Lord. Especially the apostles. They knew Jesus personally. He had called them to be apostles. Their bellies were full, they had witnessed a miracle, had fed five thousand or more people. They saw the people's insufficiency, and they saw Your sufficiency. For the moment, they had it made in the shade. You had solved a big problem.

But wait, Lord. Just a brief time earlier, they were asking You to send the people away. They saw no solution to the problem. They weren't asking You for a solution but telling You what You should do. It apparently did not cross their minds that You would have a solution.

Do I do the same thing, Lord? Do I have a problem too big for me to solve yet try to tell You how to solve it? Do I want You to fix things my way—just send the problem away, like the apostles were trying to do? Do I forget that You are sufficient, You are enough?

Forgive me, Lord, when I forget and try to control the situation. Forgive me when I feel too secure in myself, thinking I'm more important than I am, too snug like a bug in a rug. Continue to teach me to turn to You for You are sufficient. You fed five thousand plus. You can solve my little problems.

Through the all-sufficient Jesus, I pray. Amen.

So Hungry My Stomach Could Eat My Backbone

Blessed are they which do hunger and thirst after righteousness: for they shall be filled.
—Matthew 5:6 (King James Version)

Those who want to do right more than anything else are happy. God will fully satisfy them.
—Matthew 5:6 (International Children's Bible)

First, Father God, I just want to say thank you that I've never been hungry to the extent that I felt my stomach could gnaw on my backbone. Oh, I get hungry daily, but I've never been severely hungry. Even when I fasted from food, I've never been starving. There is always food around, and I can be satisfied. I am blessed.

But, You know, Lord, sometimes it is hard to know hunger. Sometimes I think I'm hungry when I'm bored. And I may think I'm hungry when I am thirsty. Other times I may be hungry and not realize it. I can ignore it when I am really focused on a goal and just go on with my life.

Is it the same way with hungering for You and Your word? Sometimes am I so focused on what I want to accomplish that I forget to get nourishment from You and Your Holy Word? Yes, I can be so intent on getting to my destination, or finishing a task, or communicating with a friend that I forget to feed myself from Your word, to talk with You, listen to You. Just like I need nourishment from food to have the protein, the vitamins, the fiber, the minerals my body needs to function at its best, I also need balanced nutrition from You for my spirit to function at its best. Other times, I'm bored and look for my nourishment from the "candy bars" of excitement or enthusiasm instead of seeking the protein and healthy fats of a good piece of fish. Afterward, I am still hungry, or hungry again very soon. It's so easy to fall into the trap of eating junk food to fill my spiritual needs instead of seeking good, nourishing food from You.

I recall the time I could hardly put one foot in front of the other. The doctors realized I was deficient in the amount of sodium in my body, so I began to drink electrolyte drinks and add salt to all my foods. Within weeks I was feeling better. It took a long time to get back to having normal energy. I think, Lord, that the same is true of my need for You. When I go too long without adequate nourishment from Your word, I become undernourished, and spiritually, I find it hard to put one foot in front of the other.

So, Lord, when I am not hungering for You or Your word, refocus me please. Help me to truly feel hunger that is enough to eat my backbone if that is what I need to return to feeding on Your word to get the spiritual nourishment I need. Thank You.

Spread like Wildfire

A bit in the mouth of a horse controls the whole horse. A small rudder on a huge ship in the hands of a skilled captain sets a course in the face of the strongest winds. A word out of your mouth may seem of no account, but it can accomplish nearly anything—or destroy it.

It only takes a spark, remember, to set off a forest fire. A careless or wrongly placed word out of your mouth can do that. By our speech we can ruin the world, turn harmony to chaos, throw mud on a reputation, send the whole world up in smoke and go up in smoke with it—smoke right from the pit of hell.

—James 3:3–6 (The Message)

That truck driver did an excellent job, Lord. He realized his big tractor-trailer rig was on fire, and he pulled it away from the building. No one got hurt, and I'm so thankful.

When I first saw it, all I saw was smoke. I questioned whether the truck was on fire. The exhaust was there, and it could have been from it. Within minutes it had flamed up, and then grabbed something that caused the flames to soar up several stories high. I feared our condominium building would catch fire. The firetrucks arrived as the explosions started and began to spray foam on it. I left the area. When I returned, less than an hour later, a shell of the truck cab remained, the trailer was black from the smoke.

Fire—it goes from a tiny spark to a big flame very rapidly, depending on the fuel, as You designed it. That's how words are, according to James in the verses above. A little word can be fuel to the fire of gossip. It can become slander. It can create hate. It can lead to riots, to the death of many, even to war.

Words. They are so important, and You want us to know that. Have I been guilty of sparks that created gossip? Or have I been guilty of saying something that was taken as slander? Have I influenced others to hate? Have my words killed the spirit of others? I need Your forgiveness for the things I've said, intentionally or unintentionally, that have hurt others. I need Your help to use my tongue to honor You by not hurting others. I need self-control, or better yet, God-control. I don't want my words to spread like wildfire. Help me to use words to accomplish good rather than create chaos or pain. Thank You.

Steel Your Spine

The servant of Elisha got up early. When he went out, he saw an army with horses and chariots all around the city. The servant said to Elisha, "Oh, my master, what can we do?"

Elisha said, "Don't be afraid. The army that fights for us is larger than the one against us."

Then Elisha prayed, "Lord, open my servant's eyes. Let him see."

The Lord opened the eyes of the young man. And he saw that the mountain was full of horses and chariots of fire all around Elisha.

—2 Kings 6:15–17
(International Children's Bible)

Suggested reading: 2 Kings 6:8–23

I love this story, Lord, because I so identify with that young man who needed to steel his spine until he saw the armies You provided. He was afraid, just as I've been afraid so many times in my life and needed to see the armies You provided, but instead I tried to steel my spine and face those fears on my own.

Thinking back over my life, I recall as a teenager the desire to be popular, and I feared people would not like me. I worked hard to learn what would make me likable. As a young adult, a fear was not getting married. Career wise, I feared not getting promotions. Later, as my career advanced, a fear was of people not being pleased with the job I did. Another fear was reprimanding people for inferior performance. I would steel my spine when I faced those fears, but I don't recall looking for Your armies until I was middle age. Sometimes even then I forgot to look to the hills for an angelic army. I wish I had.

Now, Lord, as an older adult, there are constant life fears— pain, health issues, travel, management of resources, relationships, even death. How do I face these fears? Steel my spine? Look to the hills for Your armies? It's hard to break that old habit of steeling my spine, even though experience has taught me that You have armies in the surrounding hills, ready to come to my aid, to give me peace.

Forgive me, Lord, for failing to look to You and Your armies in the past and nudge me with constant reminders to look as I face the fears of my life now and in the future. Help me see what You provide for me and help me rely on You, not myself. Steeling my spine is not nearly as comforting and reassuring as seeing Your angelic armies in the surrounding hills.

Stood Out like a Sore Thumb

But he went on asking, looking around to see who had done it. The woman, knowing what had happened, knowing she was the one, stepped up in fear and trembling, knelt before him, and gave him the whole story.

Jesus said to her, "Daughter, you took a risk of faith, and now you're healed and whole. Live well, live blessed. Be healed of your plague."
—Mark 5:32–34 (The Message)

I don't like it when I stand out like a sore thumb, Lord. They were watching the woman in this scripture story. She stuck out like a sore thumb in that crowd. She wanted to melt into the scenery, be anonymous, just be a faithful follower from a distance. She felt dirty and didn't like her body. People treated her as if she were dirty, keeping their distance from her.

You knew her real needs and what a good example she would

be for people for thousands of years to come, so You made sure her story became part of Your story.

For twelve years she had fought a blood issue. Was it some type of cancer, Lord? I don't know, but I like to think so, since I have a blood issue that is a type of cancer, although it does not cause me to bleed, but it sure causes bruising. I identify with her. Because of the rules of the time, she was not supposed to be in public for she was "unclean." I avoid the public because I don't have natural immunity. But somehow, You let her melt into the crowd, and she squeezed through all those people to get close to you and touch Your garment. She felt the instant healing. You felt the power leave Your body. Wow, I wonder what that means, but we'll talk about that another time.

She melted back into the crowd, still wanting to be anonymous. But You asked, and she finally stepped forward, feeling awkward and self-conscious, aware that the crowds were probably judging her because they considered her "unclean." You had cleansed her, and You knew the crowds needed to know—and so do we, many generations later. She needed her faith affirmed. You did it. She mattered to You.

We need our faith affirmed sometimes, Lord. I need it. You've not chosen to heal me, but to control the cancer via chemo and immunotherapy. You use people to affirm me. I feel at peace, and like this woman, You have encouraged me to "go in peace and be freed from your suffering."

I can't be anonymous with You, Lord. Yet, You don't make me stand out like a sore thumb. Even so, people watch me live, and I need to stand out for You. Help me reflect You when they look my way. Thank You.

Stop and Smell the Roses

If God gives such attention to the appearance of wildflowers—most of which are never even seen—don't you think he'll attend to you, take pride in you, do his best for you? What I'm trying to do here is to get you to relax, to not be so preoccupied with getting, so you can respond to God's giving. People who don't know God and the way he works fuss over these things, but you know both God and how he works. Steep your life in God-reality, God-initiative, God-provisions. Don't worry about missing out. You'll find all your everyday human concerns will be met.

Give your entire attention to what God is doing right now, and don't get worked up about what may or may not happen tomorrow. God will help you deal with whatever hard things come up when the time comes.

—Matthew 6:31–34 (The Message)

Cancer: it's a concerning thing, Lord.
Financial stress: it's a concerning thing, Lord.

Family members who have addictions: it's a concerning thing, Lord.

The list goes on, Lord. Yet in the middle of all the things to worry about, You remind us to stop and smell the roses. Don't get worked up, You say—cancer, finances, broken relationships, death, fears—are not what You want us to focus on. Instead, You say to stop and look with total attention at what You are doing. In earlier verses, You talk about the lilies of the fields and the birds of the air and how You care for them. You are telling us to focus on what we have, not what we don't have; You are saying that preparation is good but obsessing and worrying are not.

I'm so blessed, Lord, to look out the window into the top of a tree and see the birds that roost there, some at night including the doves that love to coo throughout the day and the mockingbirds that sing morning, noon, and evening. Some roost during the day and come out at night, including the yellow crowned and the black crowned night herons. They like to hide among the foliage. Even better at hiding is the whippoorwill, but occasionally I see him perched parallel on the limb. That's always so exciting. Watching nature is like stopping and smelling the roses for me. It reminds me that You are in control, and that old c-word, cancer, is forgotten. Thoughts of friends and loved ones with illnesses, addictions, financial woes, or other issues fade away. You are the topic of my thoughts, and when I walk away from the window, I am relaxed. I have slowed down and appreciated life.

Thank You for windows, for treetops, for foliage, for birds. The roses smell good.

Stop the World

Then Jesus took some bread. He thanked God for it, broke it, and gave it to the apostles. Then Jesus said, "This bread is my body that I am giving for you. Do this to remember me." In the same way, after supper, Jesus took the cup and said, "This cup shows the new agreement that God makes with his people. This new agreement begins with my blood which is poured out for you."

—Luke 22:19–20
(International Children's Bible)

Commune: to talk together with intensity, intimacy; interchange ideas and thoughts; associate; fellowship.

Communion: the elements of the Eucharist; the celebration of the Eucharist.

Father God, when we participate in "communion" how are we communing with You? How did the apostles, around that table with You, "commune" as they ate the bread and drank the wine that You declared to be Your body and Your blood?

When I picture the "last supper" in my mind, I see You and the twelve disciples, a baker's dozen, slowly going through the Passover meal, discussing the events of the original Passover, thus remembering what happened and why this meal was so important. You led the discussion, and each person in the room shared some part of the story. It was an important event because it brought to mind not only the events but the "whys" behind the events. It was a leisurely meal, in my imagination, with discussion among all the group and side conversations between individuals. Their worlds stopped spinning as they lay around the table discussing the occurrences of bygone years.

Were there other stories that they talked about, stories about Passovers of their childhoods? Were there memories of things their parents told them about? In my imagination, yes. I can even dream up stories Peter may have talked about his wife and mother-in-law as they celebrated Passover.

Most of our "communions" are routine experiences, where we are given or pick up a small cracker and a sip of juice or wine. Participation is not leisurely, and there is rarely conversation among the participants. There are no conversations about bygone years and special memories of our childhoods. Instead, we are encouraged to direct our thoughts toward what happened around the table You and the apostles were at and why You died a few days later on a cross. All thoughts are silent, except for the person leading the "communion service" or Eucharist. Our traditions are a lot different than the way You and the apostles did the Passover in that upper room. Our methods are efficient and hopefully we are participating to stop our little world from spinning so fast and spend a couple of minutes with our thoughts devoted to You. Is that "communing?" I hope so.

But, oh, Lord, my mind has often been somewhere besides on You. Forgive me, for I know that when I'm planning for the next week, thinking about someone I'm angry with, or daydreaming, I am not remembering You or communing with You. To commune, my thoughts must be focused on You. My little world needs to be stopped so my mind can be disciplined and concentrate on You. Otherwise, how can I commune with You?

Focusing on You during the time I participate with others in taking the bread and the wine is not easy, Lord. Teach me to better engage with You, to better commune. Help me stop the spinning world of my mind, let go of all cares and thoughts except those of You. Help me to be as focused on remembering as those apostles were when they were with You. Let my silent thoughts be of You, not worldly concerns.

Thank You, Jesus, for the bread and the wine and their representation of You, Your body that died for me, Your blood that poured out Your wounds and later Your pierced side for me. My heart hurts for You, and my mind cries out "thank You." You truly are love.

Teach an Old Dog New Tricks

Then he blessed Joseph and said,
"May the God before whom my fathers
Abraham and Isaac walked faithfully,
the God who has been my shepherd
all my life to this day,
the Angel who has delivered me from all harm
—may he bless these boys.
May they be called by my name
and the names of my fathers Abraham and Isaac,
and may they increase greatly
on the earth."
—Genesis 48:15–16
(New International Version)

Lord, Jacob didn't act like he trusted You when he was younger. He was a manipulator, doing whatever he could to get his own way, not surrendering to You. But here he says that You have been his shepherd all his life. Were You?

If so, does that mean back in the days when I was consistently trying to manipulate others and doing whatever I could to get my own way, You were my shepherd? Oh, I don't mean You wanted me to manipulate, because obviously that was not aligned with Your teachings, but does it mean that You were shepherding and guiding the results so that Jacob learned? So that I learned? Can you actually teach an old dog new tricks? If so, Lord, keep teaching this old dog some new tricks because I've made lots of mistakes in my life and need to learn to replace my old unhealthy habits with new habits that honor and glorify You.

Thank You, God of Transformation, my Transformer, my dog trainer.

Vengeance Is Mine

Dearly beloved, avenge not yourselves, but rather give place unto wrath: for it is written, Vengeance is mine; I will repay, saith the Lord.
—Romans 12:19 (King James Version)

To me belongeth vengeance and recompence, their foot shall slide in due time: for the day of their calamity is at hand, and the things that shall come upon them make haste.
—Deuteronomy 32:35 (King James Version)

Lord, I like taking things into my own hands and providing the punishment myself. And here You tell me not to. Why can't I just do it myself? It would be a lot faster. I'd get to see the person suffering. I'd feel like I'd gotten even.

I guess I need to think this through, especially since it is one of those things You bring out in both the Old and New Testaments. All my life, I've heard, "Vengeance is mine, sayeth the Lord." I knew it was Your way, but it has never felt natural.

So, what happens when I take care of the vengeance? I harbor anger. I stew over what to do to get even. I don't sleep well. My blood pressure goes up. I don't say, "I forgive you." What's more, I don't even want to forgive. I say something I later regret, maybe do something I regret also. I damage the relationship long term, not just temporarily.

That's not even pleasant, Lord. That's stuff that makes me miserable. No wonder You don't want me to be responsible for revenge. There's really nothing in it for me. But can I trust You to do it in my timing? You're so slow. At least that's how it feels. But when I reread those scriptures, You don't promise to do it in my time schedule. You just say it is Your job.

So, Lord, if I read You right, You are saying to leave the revenge to You in Your timetable. Is that better than sleepless nights, harbored anger, high blood pressure that might even lead to other problems? Probably so. Well, yes, it is.

Now I need Your help to trust You enough to do it. I understand it is a process, and I'll get there with Your guidance and the help of Your Holy Spirit. Thank You.

Watered Down

"If you want to give it all you've got," Jesus replied, "go sell your possessions; give everything to the poor. All your wealth will then be in heaven. Then come follow me."

That was the last thing the young man expected to hear. And so, crest-fallen, he walked away. He was holding on tight to a lot of things, and he couldn't bear to let go.
            —Matthew 19:21–22 (The Message)

Suggested reading: Matthew 19:16–22

Sounds like this young man wanted to go to heaven based on keeping the letter of the law, Lord, and sounds like he would have liked a watered-down gospel, not for Jesus to get to the heart of the matter. So, what can I learn from this, and what do You want of me?

If I asked You what else I need to do to go to heaven, would

You give me the same answer You gave this young man? Would You tell me to be obedient to the Ten Commandments? If so, I would also answer that I keep them, at least most of the time. I certainly was taught to follow them as a child. But if asked, "what else?" would You tell me to sell my possessions and give all to the poor? Would you question where my heart is because my lifestyle shows that I don't make any sacrifices for You, that I just comfortably go about my business and expect You to take care of me and others, and that I never show concern for others? Do I put more value in my money and my stuff than in my relationship with You?

This young man went away crestfallen, sorrowful, perhaps angry, because he wanted to hear that he was doing enough by keeping the Ten Commandments. He believed that what he did was more important than what his motives were. Do I need to examine my motives? Are they for You and pleasing You, or are they for my selfish gain? Does my pride separate me from You?

Help me, Lord, to look carefully at myself and my motives, to examine my heart, and to make some adjustments, as needed, and be willing to gladly sacrifice for You, not to care so much about my possessions. Thank You, dear Jesus, who helped this young man see the truth clearly and refused to water it down for him. Don't water it down for me either.

Thank You, God of my possessions and God of my heart.

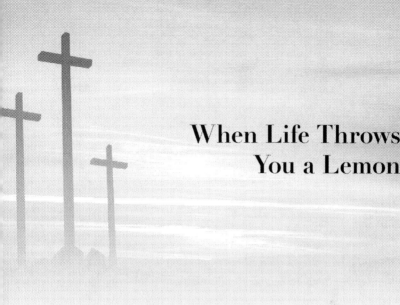

When Life Throws
You a Lemon

Turn, LORD, and deliver me;
save me because of your unfailing love.
—Psalm 6:4 (New International Version)

L ife is hard, Lord, often throwing lemons our way, making us feel sour and out-of-sorts. COVID has been hard on our society. The political environment doesn't seem healthy. Gas prices are soaring as I write this. The news media is talking about a probable recession. Health issues abound—cancer, COVID, heart attacks, strokes, food poisoning, flus, colds, Parkinson's, and the list goes on and on.

Financial woes are common with the price of housing skyrocketing, children hungry, and people simply not able to make ends meet. Pollution is a challenge, with air quality threatened, oceans contaminated with fertilizer runoff from golf courses and lawns, lakes contaminated with pesticides from farmers and mosquito control, and customers unsure of the quality of even organic fruits and vegetables. Noise pollution bombards our thoughts.

The hardest of all, Lord, may be relationship problems. These lead us to misery so often. We divorce our spouses, put distance between our parents and ourselves, try to control our children, complain about our neighbors, find fault in church members, and lack patience with store clerks. We lay awake at night thinking of how we could have done something differently, how we could have reacted, sometimes trying to talk to You but our minds wandering off to our selfish wishes.

Health, finances, relationships … yes, there are lemons in life. But You, Lord, can deliver us. And You are willing.

How can we be delivered? By seeking Your help. Asking for it. Trusting You to deliver us. As the psalmist prayed in Psalm 6:4, we need to ask You to turn toward us, deliver us. Oh, I've done that many times by telling You how I wanted You to deliver me. But that's not my job. I need to surrender my will to You, not give You the solution. You are far more creative than me, and You can much more easily find the absolute best way out of the demanding situation. After all, You have the big picture. I don't.

Why do You do this? Because of Your "unfailing love." The Hebrew word "hesed" doesn't translate well into our English language, but the idea is that You do it because of Your loving kindness, Your attachment to us in love, an unfailing love. That's more than we can imagine, but there is no lemon ever thrown to us in this life on earth that Your "hesed" can't deal with. It's perfect love.

Lord, teach us to surrender, to seek You and Your "hesed." Thank You.

Wolf in Sheep's Clothing

But Jesus put it right back on them. "Why do you use your rules to play fast and loose with God's commands? God clearly says, 'Respect your father and mother,' and, 'Anyone denouncing father or mother should be killed.'"
—Matthew 15:3–5 (The Message)

Jesus knew what they were thinking, and said, "Why this gossipy whispering?"
—Matthew 9:4 (The Message)

I've noticed, Lord, that You asked a lot of questions when You were on earth. You used them to get people to think. You used them often with the Pharisees, who would ask questions of You first, usually trying to corner You into answering their way. Sometimes You made it clear by Your questions that You considered many of them to be wolves in sheep's clothing, They didn't practice what they preached, so their inside thoughts and attitudes didn't match their outside appearances.

When I notice those questions, I too often try to ignore that You are also asking them of me, even asking more personal questions of me. What would You ask me, Lord, if I tried to get You to clarify the rules we follow about the commandment "Thou shall have no other gods"? Maybe You would ask me about my allegiance to the church, giving more honor to the institution than to You? Would You ask me about why I seek to impress people, forgetting to seek to impress You? Oh, I don't like this one, but You would ask me about why I judge people in my thoughts, placing my ideas of what is important above my love for them. Would you ask me about why I have so many clothes in my closet? Might it be about why I avoid fasting because I don't want to sacrifice a little food every now and then? Would you ask me why it is so much easier to fast a meal than it is to fast my appearances or my apathy or my stinginess?

You know, Lord, You could get me on those and many other things, for I am often a wolf in sheep's clothing. Help me recognize when I do these things, to ask for Your forgiveness (and if I've offended someone or done wrong by them, to ask for their forgiveness also) and to seek Your help to change, to be transformed, as Paul suggests in Romans 12:1–2. Thank You for loving the Pharisees enough to make them aware that they were being wolves in sheep clothing. Thank You for loving me enough to know when I am also acting like a clean white sheep but internally feeling like a wolf with a grin on his face because he has just devoured someone. I can change with the help of Your Holy Spirit.

You Reap What You Sow

Don't be misled: No one makes a fool of God. What a person plants, he will harvest. The person who plants selfishness, ignoring the needs of others—ignoring God—harvests a crop of weeds. All he'll have to show for his life is weeds. But the one who plants in response to God, letting God's Spirit do the growth work in him, harvests a crop of real life, eternal life.

—Galatians 6:7–8 (The Message)

Like Paul said, Lord, You are not a fool. You are omnipotent, omniscient, omnipresent. Those are big words just to say You have all power, You are all knowing, You are everywhere. You know what is going on with my friend whose husband is telling her it is her fault that he's drinking too much. That's a lie, Lord, and You know it. But Lord, he's told that lie to her for so many years that she believes it. Yet she also knows it's not true. Her head knows it is not, but her reactions are habitual, and she lives as if it is true, beating up on herself, blaming herself for things for which she has no responsibility.

Eventually, Lord, he's going to reap what he has sown, with night after night of heavy drinking, vomiting, peeing on himself, falling, sleeping on the floor because he's too inebriated to get to the bed. Then he smokes marijuana to try to get rid of the effects of the alcohol. It's a viscous cycle. Yet he loves You. He's caught in the cycle Paul describes in Romans 7. So is she. For him, it is addiction. For her, it is blame and guilt.

Yet there is a difference in the two, Lord. She's seeing a counselor, getting help, learning to be honest with herself and You. He denies that he has a problem, refuses to go to AA or Celebrate Recovery. He claims that he can stop drinking anytime he wants to. But look at what happens, Lord: he might skip a night or even several to prove he can not drink, but then he gets drunk again. She must hide the keys, so he won't drive and possibly kill someone. What a messy life …

Yet, Lord, You are working. You are helping her to get the backbone to face the demons that have controlled her for so long. She's learning to stand up to him, and not let him blame her for his failures. You've put people in his life to pray for him. That gives me hope. Maybe someday he too will change. Meantime, Lord, teach him by the harvest he is reaping from the seeds he has sown and is sowing. Help him become honest with himself and You. Make him into a man after Your own heart.

Continue, Lord, to teach her, and guide her to practice tough love, to be willing to live alone if that is what she needs to do to glorify and honor You. Erase the lies she believes and replace them with Your truths, for we know that truth sets us free.

What a mess, Lord, but You are God of messes. You've fixed lots of them. I pray this through the power of Jesus, who was raised from the dead. You created the principle of reaping what we sow. You have the power and I trust You to fix this mess. Thank You.

Your Neck of the Woods

And the second is like to this: Thou shalt love thy neighbor as thyself.
>   —Matthew 22:39 (Douay-Rheims
>   1899 American Edition)

But he willing to justify himself, said to Jesus: And who is my neighbor?
>   —Luke 10:29 (Douay-Rheims
>   1899 American Edition)

Every version that I've looked at, Lord, has said the same thing: love your neighbor as yourself. The rich young ruler that You told the story about in the Luke scripture is the same, no matter the version, too—he wants to know who his neighbor is. So do I, Lord. Who is my neighbor?

There are my "next-door neighbors"—obviously, they are my neighbors. They live in "my neck of the woods." But the man by the road in the story of the good Samaritan didn't live next door. The good Samaritan didn't know him. He was a stranger, from a different culture. He had physical needs. You said that it was good to take care of him, even though he was from a different neck of the woods.

With the internet today, Lord, we have access to people around the world. We know needs of folks from every culture, or at least we can find out their needs. So, are they our neighbors? How do we go about helping them? What about those folks we read about in *Voice of the Martyrs* magazine? Their stories make us cry. How can we be neighbors to them? They are in a different neck of the woods, but we care.

What about those folks in war-torn countries? We see them on the television news, read about them on internet news. What role do you want us to take, since we are not really in their neck of the woods? How can we be good neighbors from half a world away?

The homeless, Lord—am I to treat them as neighbors? Those that are in jail—how can I treat them as neighbors? I don't even want to be in their neck of the woods, if I'm honest, Lord. Yet by the example of the good Samaritan, I'm their neighbor and I've got a job to do.

Keep teaching and transforming me, Lord, so that I am more willing to love my neighbor as myself. I need Your Holy Spirit to work through me because I'm a lot like the rich young ruler, just wanting to go off and keep doing what I've always done. I want to be justified. My heart needs You to change it. Thank You.

Printed in the United States
by Baker & Taylor Publisher Services